The Red Pencil

Theodore R. Sizer

The Red Pencil

Convictions from Experience in Education

YALE UNIVERSITY PRESS • NEW HAVEN AND LONDON

Designed by Nancy Ovedovitz and typeset in Monotype Fournier by Duke & Company.

Printed in the United States of America by R. R. Donnelley & Sons.

The Library of Congress has cataloged the hardcover edition as follows:
Sizer, Theodore R.
The red pencil : convictions from experience in education / Theodore R. Sizer.
p. cm.
ISBN 0-300-10458-8 (cloth : alk. paper)
1. Education, Secondary—United States. 2. Sizer, Theodore R.
I. Title.LA222.S546 2004
373.73—dc22   2004045645

A catalogue record for this book is available from the British Library.

The paper in this book meets the guidelines for permanence and durability of the Committee on Production Guidelines for Book Longevity of the Council on Library Resources.

ISBN 0-300-10977-6 (pbk. : alk. paper)

10   9   8   7   6   5   4   3   2   1

The forcible writer stands bodily behind his words with his experience—He does not make books out of books, but he has been *there* in person.
—Henry David Thoreau (1842)

Contents

Preface: The Red Pencil

I was fourteen and a tenth grader in high school when I first tackled "second-year" Latin. Our instructor was our school's most celebrated scholar-teacher, Joseph Barrell. Behind his back, we called him "Joe." To his face, it was "Sir" or "Mister Barrell," titles expected in a traditional school in 1946.

I had experienced "first-year" Latin in various gentle forms in my elementary school and during my initial year at the Pomfret School, the then-all-male boarding school in northeastern Connecticut where I was to confront Joe Barrell. Throughout, I had struggled. Latin, especially Latin grammar, was for me terra incognita, in spite of the persistent ministrations of warm-hearted Classics teachers in seventh, eighth, and ninth grades. I knew that Joe would be a challenge for me. I devoutly hoped that I would not be a challenge for him.

Insensitively, perhaps, the dozen or so of us in our class never recognized much warmth in Joe's heart. He was to our eyes an "old" teacher (when, in fact, he was a Yale graduate student in English finishing his Ph.D. thesis on Percy Bysshe Shelley and his circle). The "oldness" arose from his formality and formidable intellect. His teacher's desk was on a low platform backed against a chalkboard, facing several high windows. He looked down at us. Before him were rows of bolted-down flip-top wooden desks, most of them festooned with small carvings clandestinely engraved by long past predecessor Latin and Greek students. Fading prints of ancient poets and historians furbished the walls.

We started with Caesar (or was it Cornelius Nepos?). Barrell set a prescribed number of lines each night. In class the next day he would randomly pick some boy to start off with the translation of the first assigned sentence. If that unlucky leadoff batter came close to providing an accurate rendition, Joe moved in order along that student's row demanding that the next sentence be translated. If, on the other hand, the first boy had struck out, or clearly had done little of the homework, the second boy had to tackle the sentence that the first had bollixed. This being the daily routine, once Joe had signaled which boy in which row was to open the translation, we all had a fair idea of just when our time to perform would come. We could not easily identify the precise sentence that we would have to confront, as we never surely knew who might flub and have his sentence passed along. We calculated nonetheless, making quick judgments of the likelihood that each particular student would or would not deliver to Joe's satisfaction. We waited, clammy with anticipation, for the moment of our judgment.

What really riveted our attention, however, was Joe's grade book, or, more accurately, the pencil he used to inscribe his judgment of our performances in a small, bound ledger. Barrell would say, "Barnes, translate," listen carefully, and then record a grade. We became experts (we believed) in tracking the movement of his pencil. A. Or B–. Or—please, please make it not be so!—E. By the end of class we all, save the few Classics Hot Shots, were ready to explode with tension.

That pencil and its penalties remain with me as a painful token of my battle both with Latin and with the notion that my struggles could be so neatly reduced to a cold expression, say a D, in Joseph Barrell's little book. Class with Joe was a place to show off in one prescribed way what we had done on our own. We all were held to precisely the same narrow standard (*agricolam* is in the accusative case or it isn't), and the daily test was the translation of Latin into coherent English. Joe did give some brief lectures on the context of the texts, but the action that counted was all in precise decoding. And so that pencil became my torturer. It was unrelenting in its impersonality.

Many years later my wife, Nancy, pinned a small drawing and a bit of poetry over the desk at which she spent endless weekends grading high school history papers, a winsome piece she had discovered in the *New York Times*. The cartoon depicts a gnome-ish man with a long, pointed nose. The title is "The Red Pen." The text is by R. F. Pease: "It slides swiftly across paper, brushing errors off the page— it strikes terror into punctuation. Red ink acts with accuracy, finding fault, doing its job." Joseph Barrell insisted on accuracy, finding fault when error reared its head. That was his job.

What is most interesting about Joe's memorable class more than fifty years later—infinitely more relevant than my childish terror— is how remarkably familiar it yet is, especially in settled, well-financed, well-regarded secondary schools provided for America's economically secure families and generally sought after by most families. Some details are now quaint: the segregation by sex, the raised platform, the formality, the individual flip-top wooden desks in rows, the unvarying pedagogy, the considerable fear that a teacher could then provoke. What is remarkable, however, is that so much of the 1946 regimen is still with us.

Most of it is not only recognizable; it is still fully accepted and honored today as a representation of what we call secondary school: *a class* of twenty or so adolescents gathered by age into *grades* to learn *together* a *subject* both for its *content* and for the *skills* embedded in that content taught by a *single teacher* who is responsible for *delivering* that material, assigning *homework*, and *assessing* each student's performance in a uniform manner, all this proceeding in sequential *blocks of time* of forty to sixty minutes each in a specialized *school building* primarily made up of a succession of identical rooms that are used for six hours for fewer than half the days in a year. Joe Barrell would not feel wholly lost in any college preparatory program at any school, public or private, large or small, in Connecticut or beyond, in 2004. This is what *school* is.

What makes the persistence of this routine even more interesting is that its effectiveness has long been known to be weak, "effectiveness" defined as the students' ultimate resourceful use of the content and skills being studied. Nonetheless, the form of such a "good" school is still widely accepted, and today's students assembled in classes akin to Joe Barrell's surely have palms as sweaty as mine were. The red pencil has, perhaps, been replaced by the machine-graded standardized test, a trivial difference. Tradition in the framework of schooling has remarkable momentum.

There is great strength in tradition, especially if it provides what a culture needs in a fair and practical manner. Today's secondary schools largely fail to meet that standard. The best predictor of a child's educational success always has been and still is the economic and social class of his family rather than the school that he or she happens to attend. The schools as they presently function appear, save at the well-publicized margins, rarely to countervail the accidents of family, wealth, and residence. "Success," as conventionally defined, and ultimately graduation thus depend largely on the chance of birth and income, embarrassing a democracy that pretends to offer equal educational opportunities for all.

Further, school, as Americans conduct it, is expensive. Its buildings, equipment, and staff are engaged only part of the year. Few private businesses could survive long with so much downtime of costly infrastructure. On top of this is the fact that the children of poorer families —presumably youngsters who might require more support—are generally found in the less supportive settings. The same classes are still offered, but they have forty-five rather than twenty students (on the rolls at least; truancy is an epidemic in many high schools). Mr.

Barrell's successor is there, but he knows far less about his subject than he wishes he knew, and he has taught only a few years. The tensions of the street spill over into his classroom, making a search for the accusative of *agricola* almost absurd in such an atmosphere; his school is likely to be very large and, thereby, for all but unusually confident kids, scary in its noisy complexity and cold in its unavoidable anonymity.

This American paradox—an often maudlin worship of the idea of universal schooling and a very faint heart in making it deserve that worship—puzzled me over my entire academic and professional career. The fact that we shy away from its hard realities is fascinating. It is not that we do not talk about them, research them, and exhort "leaders" to address them. It is that we largely fail to marshal the honesty and intensity that reform requires.

I have pondered secondary education for almost five decades as the spouse of a high school teacher; as a parent of four and a grandparent of ten; as a teacher and principal in four secondary schools, in both private and public sectors in the United States and Australia; as a scholar, university faculty member, teacher trainer, and Education school dean; as a full-time field researcher and school designer; and as a member of a variety of committees at local, state, and national levels. I know elementary schools well enough to know that they are beset by many but, happily, not all of the costly eccentricities of secondary schools. This book centers largely on the latter.

I have been a school watcher long enough to observe California's public schools sink from pre–Proposition 13 prominence to their current disastrous condition; I know firsthand what that great state has lost. I have broken bread with New York City school Chancellors from Calvin Gross in 1964 to Harold Levy in 2001; I know how similar were the challenges faced by Gross and Levy. Over the past two decades I have visited scores of schools in more than a dozen states. I have sat on myriad commissions that have examined the educational status quo, and I have experienced déjà vu in our recommendations.

Throughout I have always been close enough to adolescents to find them interesting, often sage, often colorful, never dull, eager to glom on to the latest fashion or technology, unrealistic in their belief that each is immune to danger, most, however naively, hopeful. I have been extraordinarily blessed by the gift of a richly varied professional life.

In reflecting on this life I have been struck as much by the silences hovering around talk of education as by the noise of its familiar working. For decades we have focused mostly on the same things: the definition of the curriculum; the ways and means of funding schools; the roles of parent, teacher, principal, superintendent, commissioner, governor, president; teacher education; "leadership"; assessment; incentives or shame to drag schools into better performance. Over the past one hundred years, the basic framework of the school system, including the meanings attached to the words describing it, have endured, with little challenge. No word is more quickly—silently—accepted, for example, than *system*, implying in this context that learning can be shaped into predictable behavior and thus predictable, equitable, and efficient performance as long as we have a well-defined and imposable scheme to direct our activities.

Unquestionably, efficiency is gained by cleaving to such familiar words as "system" and the practices that flow from them. The danger is that they narrow our imagination. At worst, they cripple our work.

Evasion

After a day's visit, I talk with the principal of a typical American junior-senior high school, a good and proud one in the eyes of its community. The principal is an old friend. After pleasantries, we start jousting.

"We agree that neither you nor I can teach any student well whom we do not know well," I begin.

"Yes. You gotta know 'em."

"Your English teachers carry each semester a load of 120 kids, more over the entire year. How can you realistically expect them to know so many kids well enough to teach each of them well?"

Silence.

"And you chop up the day of each student into forty-seven-minute blocks. With the incessant coming and going, that means maybe forty minutes, max. How well do you learn tough stuff in forty-minute snatches sandwiched between other equally rushed matters?"

Silence.

"It doesn't make sense, any sense at all. Common sense."

"I know."

"So, do something about it."

"I can't."

"Why not?"

"They wouldn't let me. It would be too different."

"Can't you even talk about it?"

"No. They do not want to hear about that sort of stuff."

"Why not?"

"They just don't. It would open a can of worms."

I am aware that professional education's silences—the failure to think freshly about the practical implications of crucial words and all-too-familiar practices, for example—are not the products of inattention. Most of us recognize and acknowledge them, however obliquely. Nonetheless, we—from experienced principals to the layered bureaucracies towering above them—leave them be.

We dare not address them. To fill those silences with policy and practice—to take seriously what we know about who our children are, how they learn, and what is necessary to forward that learning—would profoundly upset the system with which we are comfortable and which serves many families and professional educators reasonably well. To rethink what it is to create an intelligent and free citizenry—to fill the most troublesome silences—is a formidable political challenge.

In this book I wish to ponder three of these silences.[1]

The first rests in the difference between teaching and learning. Teaching implies a place where educators provide a service for a child, within the walls of a school building. Learning reflects what that child is ingesting from all sources, not just those arising from teacherly ministrations.

If we care about what adolescents are actually learning, we must look within and far beyond school buildings, at "the street" and especially at the modern information-rich and incessantly commercial culture within which we exist. Formal education—schooling—has to adapt to and confront the exceedingly powerful education found beyond traditional classrooms. This reality has been obvious for decades. Save for passionate essays here and little add-on programs there, we have dodged its implications. Doing good things in a building called school is not enough. It shows.

The second addresses authority, what it is and who has the right to wield it. We know a great deal about power, but power and authority are not necessarily the same things. By focusing on who is organizationally In Charge, we neglect the complex matter of who deserves to be in charge, why, and how. Who owns a child's mind? The family? The community? If the community, which community? The neighborhood? The city? The state? The nation?

Does authority rest solely with whatever agency spends money? Is management of resources the only legitimate expression of authority?

The currently familiar privatization and choice debates and the imposition of abrupt, one-shot assessments, whether Joe Barrell's pencil or a high-stakes standardized test, dodge too much of the matter. When a free society *compels* its citizens to do something, like attend school in order to achieve a specific result, the hand of the state needs to be informed, restrained, and nuanced. One person's authority over another places a burden on both. Although there is awareness of these issues, there is almost universal silence within the education system, its practitioners, and its policy makers over what authority in fact is and how—in a democracy at least—it is responsibly wielded. The silence is costly and undermines the legitimacy of the entire process of public education.

The third silence arises from our fetish with order, our belief that imposed systems will bring education to the people. Systems are important, but they are a means, not an end, and even then "systems" are only one kind of means. American formal education—in the way it functions and describes itself—is the principal institutional residue of the early twentieth-century factory system. School is as school was; the astonishingly durable "grammar" of schooling, the nature of "real school," the regularities of schooling have been repeatedly identified and challenged.[2] We know that. We usually deplore it, but when we "reform" our school systems we leave most of their familiar routines undisturbed. To shake up the system that fills the time of children and adolescents, thus keeping them out of the home and the labor market, apparently is too dangerous to contemplate. Silence reigns.

All of these silences are familiar. All have been studied. Much has been written about each. I admire many of these inquiries, and I have learned from them. I am respectful of how little effect most of them have had both on school practice and on policy.

I am encouraged by the recently renewed interest in educational research but am disappointed both in its scope, one now dominated by the social, behavioral, and increasingly the biological sciences, and in the apparent indifference to the question of how the results of research might affect the taut complexities of schools. Further, matters of mass education are not only technical and procedural; they are also cultural and philosophical. The influence of humanistic disciplines is hard to discover in contemporary research planning. Finally, most current discussion assumes that research results will lead to detailed practices that will feed into the existing system—the very system that research has shown to be greatly flawed.

I respect traditional scholarly research, and I have made my own contributions to its corpus. I respect the many friends that I have in our school systems who are trying to get us from today to a better tomorrow.

Although I am attentive to existing scholarly work, my fifty years of experience have nudged me to try to look beyond the familiar touchstones of education and to speculate about what I see. Accordingly, my primary approach in this book is to go beyond well-recognized texts and analyses and to draw mainly from my own experience, "experience" defined as both what I learned as a practitioner as well as what I learned from books and at the feet of thoughtful people.

Accordingly, this is neither a how-to book nor a philippic against any particular group. It focuses on truths we all too often and none too gracefully dodge. I call them "silences." *The Red Pencil* is an argument wrapped in a memoir, a brief of convictions about growing up and learning, about "school," that rests on the evidence from experience, of actions taken, of books read, and of influential friends met.

Memory

My Latin with Joe Barrell became even more treacherous after Caesar (or Nepos). We had a bit of Ovid and of Horace, but the killer was the Vulgate (Latin) version of the Gospel according to John. At least Caesar's battles in Gaul were comprehensible. John's Gospel was utterly impregnable to most of us even in English (we all had run quickly to Bibles to check it out). We learned much about getting through class and trying to influence that red pencil but few of us gained much technical—not to mention literary or historical—knowledge about Latin. What primarily sticks with me to this day is fear.

Mr. Barrell remains a powerful, if unbeloved, figure for me. Looking back now, he represents some of the glory and much of the misdirection of traditional education.

Barrell was a scholar; he knew his stuff. Academically, he was always a bit over our heads, including those of the Hot Shots, a worthy tactic. He kept the pressure on us to do careful work regularly. The symbols in his little book were evidence that he was paying attention to us, at least as Latin translators, one by one. When a few of us (myself in the lead) were drastically failing he arranged for tutoring from his wife, also a Classics scholar, whose style was warmer and gentler, albeit no less demanding, than was his. Most importantly, even at the cool distance from which he addressed us and from the narrow perch from which he assessed us, he took us seriously.

I can see him now, blue work shirt with wool tie, books orderly before him as he sat at his desk, calm, exhibiting no strong emotion. Most else of what I did in school leaves no such detailed image; I cannot recite even the titles of all the courses that I took. What I remember is selective but stark and detailed, retained not for any abiding joy in the Classics but for the simple reason that Barrell terrified me.

Apart from inflicting the memorable terror, Barrell never led us to invade the Classics deeply, to get beyond the syntax, to see the constancy of humanity in its passions and its terrors, to understand that constancy, and thereby be inspired to grasp the habit of reading serious books from a serious past, to persuade us that immersion in such texts could be a lifelong enriching joy. He rarely ascertained *why* we made a mistake, much less helped us to correct it; he served primarily as a scorekeeper, sorting the proper from the improper. Latin with Barrell was a chore, an annoying but temporary thing like washing dishes supervised by a nitpicky older sister. It was something we had to do because this was School.

Such memories form mental images, tableaus that sway over time, toned both by subsequent events and by the erosion inevitable with the passage of years. A few powerfully endure, and whether I like it or not they shape the way that I see the world, in the case of this book my professional world and the silences that I now sense within it.

I am sure that such recollecting is not an unusual habit. Remembrances influence each of us and direct our enthusiasms and fears. Most of my recollecting is inevitably myopic, involving intense events that mean much to me but are legitimately trivial to others. They are shards of experience, such as a recitation for Joseph Barrell and so much that came later.

My intent in this book is to bring a design to some of these shards, to gather those that appear to transcend my particular backyard and to arrange them, without any strict discipline of chronology or familiar classification, in ways that provide meaning, and to ponder how these combinations give rise to my convictions, ones that reflect a special interest in three important "silences," of a recognition of what we are *not* doing, *not* talking about, *not* experiencing, at least not enough, on behalf of the learning by children.

I share this personal effort in the hope that it may be usefully provocative for others, especially those who attend to the learning of youth, encouraging them to reflect on and make practical meaning of their own experiences, to find the silences in their own work, and to fill those silences with thought and action.

I   Building

Many of my friends work in high schools. Many of these are principals, the people ultimately in charge of their domains. Many of them call themselves "building principals," and I am so used to this labeling that I take it for granted. What they—and I, for a decade in two places—were responsible for was a *building*, and its precious human occupants. The first word in that compound noun referred to a structure. It was not a gerund, speaking of people who create or constructed schools. Rather, we were the principals of physical places.

In a subtle but telling way this characterization outlines the range and limits of our responsibilities as principals, and, given the way school systems currently work, makes sense. We educators are to deliver good skills and worthy ideas to children in a prescribed, appropriately laid out space. School is, then, something like a thoughtful store that all of a certain age are required to patronize.

The problem is that what we principals believe we provide may not be fully deliverable in the stores that we operate. High schools alone cannot do the job assigned them.

Sleepy

I sat in on an "advisory" (a "homeroom" period) at a large senior high school in a small, desperately poor East Coast industrial city. Although one of the purposes of the session was to take attendance, the gathering was not the first formal "period" of the day. Kids stumbled into the school slowly during the early morning hours, and if attendance had been taken at this beginning of the day, the list sent to central headquarters would show many truants. The numbers grew slowly during the morning, and it made good political sense to count noses mid-morning rather than at the day's start.

The classroom in the grand but fearfully neglected schoolhouse found a scattering of tablet chairs haphazardly gathered into small clusters. The teacher, an amiable and assured person, waved me in; she was working at her desk. More than a dozen kids, all probably sixteen or seventeen, slouched together, still draped on this chilly morning in various forms of warm dress. Massive backpacks for each were piled nearby. As there was apparently no organized activity going on, I chose the quartet of kids nearest the door and asked if I could join them. Without much expression but with no complaint, they welcomed me to their company.

Two were girls, both Latinas, probably from families recently arrived from the Dominican Republic. One was well turned out, confident and articulate, the other, much in her shadow, less so but watching and listening carefully. One of the boys was Caucasian, festooned with piercing and jewelry from ears to eyelids to nose to lower lip. He was frantically writing, copying from scrawls on a piece of notebook paper. He muttered to me and to no one in general that if he did not have this report ready for some class he was in some sort of trouble. I soon learned that the paper from which he was copying was the homework of Ms. Confident. It had been plucked from a mess of papers that had been in front of her, all piled together helter-skelter, soon to be jammed back into her backpack. The other male, probably

Dominican-American, was head down on the tablet of his desk, awake but visibly exhausted.

The two girls were up for chatting. What grade were they in? Eleventh. What courses were they taking? Math. English. Science. The list was familiar. One had Dance, which she enjoyed. What were they thinking about doing after graduating next year? College. Which colleges are you looking at? There was silence. Then, "Harvard." Why Harvard? I don't know. Have you visited any colleges? No. What would you like to study in college? Science. Both wanted to be doctors, but Ms. Less Confident seemed dubious about her chances. Ms. Confident told me that she had only one credit to collect as a senior; she was already that close to her diploma. She admitted to one additional hurdle, however: she had repeatedly failed the state's standardized required tenth-grade-level test in mathematics.

Do you have jobs after school? Both replied yes. What were they? Clerking. Working with elders. Babysitting. Do you work most days? Yes, every day. There was no complaint in this admission; it was spoken as though regular work-for-pay was routine, during the week as well as on the weekends. Neither mentioned any extracurricular, beyond-the-school-day obligations like activity clubs.

Mr. Pierced Head was clearly not one to question. He was writing with a fury, but with a smile on his face. I turned to Mr. Sleepy. Again, an eleventh grader. Yes, he would go to college. Where? He did not know. Any places that you might consider? He had no names to suggest. Do you have a job? Yes, two jobs. Where? I work in a nursing home after school. How many days? Five. How many hours a day? Six. And the other job? Weekends. Where? UPS. Hours? Eight hours both days.

The principal later told me about this small city. It was poor but rents were high. Most of the kids came from "the Islands," meaning primarily Puerto Rico and the Dominican Republic. Extended families shared rented quarters, with all family members in their teens and older earning money to pay the bills. Even in such financial straits, many family members, including school-aged kids, returned for short or extended periods to the Caribbean. The principal told me of frequent comings and goings, with students suddenly absent for weeks at a time and, equally as suddenly, reappearing in school. Year to year the school's roster changed; last year's kids were nominally present this year in some numbers, but it was impossible to plan very sensibly. "Eleventh grade" had only chronological meaning.

The principal and the teachers, largely Caucasian and veteran, clearly loved these adolescents, even the toughest of the lot, and worked hard within the arrangements that they had inherited to help them. Their city was crime-infested and long corrupt. Most of the students scored poorly on the state's standardized tests; this had to be no surprise. The school's year-to-year aggregated comparative scores showed little movement, again not surprisingly; the churning turnover of students made this almost inevitable. The school was frequently speared, even ridiculed, in the press. And yet these adults carried on, even in the face of the aspersion, with pride in the hard-bought progress their kids were making.

Ambitious redesign of the high school was under way, led by a new superintendent brought in from another city. State government was carrying a substantial load of the school's costs; the city had a tax base incapable of supporting its families—families that provided most of the economically necessary low-level, low-salary workforce for the factories and businesses in the suburbs.

This school represents much of what is wrong with American public education. It is a wide-held belief that the lives of children like these can be dramatically improved by what happens inside of a grand, shabby old building like theirs. In fact, over the course of a year, most children spend more than twice their waking hours outside of school. This time, not surprisingly, carries far more influence than the amount of time spent in the classroom, if not for some, surely for most.

The four teenagers with whom I shared a bit of an "advisory" personify that reality. Their plight is not a secret and has become the subject of endless criticism and mockery in the press and in the halls of power. Criticism of public education is now a big, noisy, self-righteous industry.

A great *silence*, however, surrounds the most sensible, indeed stunningly obvious, remedy in support of these children: policy and practice that spread over the traditional but separate public services—educational, social, medical, financial—and create a seamless support and ministering system. Today's professional entities, now largely in institutional isolation—education, social work, economic development, public housing, public safety, and more—demonstrably fail, being less than their combined parts. We early twenty-first-century Americans seem so paralyzed by the routines of what is now "in place" to help children that we fail to see what is completely obvious: if we want a powerfully educated population we must attend to all aspects of each child's situation, in deliberate, sustained combination.

The Forming of Society

This obvious but largely ignored fact had surfaced for me forty years earlier in the rarified atmosphere of the Harvard Graduate School of Arts and Sciences, where I was at work toward a Ph.D. in Education and American History. My graduate school adviser Bernard Bailyn's *Education in the Forming of American Society: Needs and Opportunities for Study* had been published by the University of North Carolina Press in 1960, just as I was starting my thesis research. Although colonial institutions were miles away from modern city school systems, the way that one *thought* about deliberate education, the way that one might usefully define both "deliberate" and "education," whether in the eighteenth century or later, is timeless. If education is defined as the expressed intelligence of the people, one gets to a different place than if education is defined as what government provides to deliver ideas, skills, and attitudes to the people. The difference is not trivial. Bailyn's book profoundly affected the way I have come to perceive my work.

Bailyn's slim volume had followed a conference on popular learning sponsored by the Institute of Early American History and Culture at Williamsburg and consisted of an interpretation of the definition and meaning of education in the colonial period followed by a critical listing and assessment of relevant documents. Although my scholarly studies in the late 1950s were drifting toward an interest in the education of youth in the late national period, Bailyn's analysis was provocative to me then as a historian and later as someone trying to make sense of the world of schools and the learning of adolescents, more particularly of what the former might usefully provide for the latter.

Bailyn wrote critically about the historians of the late nineteenth and early twentieth centuries. "The main emphasis and ultimately the main weakness of the history written by the educational missionaries of the turn of the [twentieth] century derived from their professional interests. Seeking to demonstrate the immemorial importance and evolution of the theories and procedures of the work in which they were engaged, they directed their attention almost exclusively to the part of the educational process carried on in formal institutions of instruction. They spoke of schools as self-contained entities whose development had followed an inner logic and an innate propulsion." Bailyn suggested a better vantage point for scholars, urging them to assume "a broader definition of education and a different notion of historical relevance. It becomes apparent when one thinks of education not only as a formal pedagogy but as the entire process by which a culture transmits itself across the generations; when one is prepared to see great variations in the role of formal institutions of instruction, to see schools and universities fade into relative insignificance next to other social agencies; when one sees education in its elaborate, intricate involvements with the rest of society, and notes its shifting functions, meanings, and purposes."[1]

"Fundamental change," Bailyn continued, "may be seen only . . . when one assumes that the past was not incidentally but essentially different from the present; when one seeks as the points of greatest relevance those critical passages of history where elements of our familiar present, still part of an unfamiliar past, begin to disentangle themselves, begin to emerge amid confusion and uncertainty. For these soft, ambiguous moments where the words we use and the institutions we know are notably present but are still enmeshed in older meanings and different purposes—these are the moments of true origination. They reveal in purest form essential features which subsequent events complicate and modify but never completely transform."[2]

In the title of his book, Bailyn makes the bold but persuasive argument that education—defined as the forces enculturating youth and arising from a tangle of formal and informal agencies—*forms* a society. We Americans are what our congeries of influential agencies make —that is *teach*—us. To tackle just one of those entities independently, whether the high school, the family, the media, the labor market, or whatever, is to miss the crux of the matter, which is that youth ultimately reflect the inevitable braiding of these influences on their lives.

Education is more than schooling, but schooling does affect the culture, for good or ill, in some respect. Although Bailyn's scholarly essay was devoted to the historiography of early American education, its general message has persistently discomfited me. While zeroing in on "school reform," as I have tried to do in recent decades, has been practical (no one can do everything at once) and politically acceptable to governments and philanthropy, in the long run, it makes limited sense. The narrow "inside-of-school" focus, however comfortable, has been and surely still is wrong-headed. Traditionally inward-focused and autonomous schools are unlikely to "form" much of importance in this roaring early twenty-first-century society. If well designed, these institutions can help; but, given our information- and image-rich culture, they are unlikely to be the most consequential players in the lives of their students, whether economically secure white children or poor immigrants from "the Islands."

A Matter of Class

Schools are important, but only to the extent that they are part of a larger, thoughtful pattern. One does not understand early American education without attending to such a pattern, as Bailyn argued in 1960. Eight years later, while I was yet at Harvard, these convictions were deepened by the deliberations of a complement of social scientists gathered in Cambridge by Daniel Patrick Moynihan.

Moynihan came to Harvard in July 1966 as Professor of Education and Urban Politics and Director of the Harvard-MIT Joint Center for Urban Studies. The possibility of his joining us was presented to me, then the Education School's Dean, by James Q. Wilson, then an Associate Professor of Government at Harvard and the Center's Acting Director. Its previous Director, Robert Wood, had been called by the Johnson administration to serve in the Department of Housing and Urban Development. I had earlier worked with Wilson as part of a project sponsored by the Task Force on Economic Growth and Opportunity, primarily by writing a chapter on schooling for a book, *The Metropolitan Enigma: Inquiries into the Nature and Dimensions of America's "Urban Crisis,"* which Wilson was editing.[3]

Moynihan, then a Fellow at Wesleyan University and a man steeped in knowledge of the American urban scene, might be available, Wilson said. He implied that Moynihan was not likely to be accepted by Harvard's Government Department, perhaps because he had been too recently an activist (and a controversial one, given the 1965 release of a politically grating paper for the U.S. Department of Labor entitled "The Negro Family: The Case for National Action") and not a career scholar in the accepted Arts and Sciences tradition. Wilson knew of the Education School's vigorous effort to connect, in ways appropriate to a professional school, with reform in cities. Could Moynihan find a place with us? My Education colleagues and I believed that he could.

Such an appointment to tenure was no easy thing in the 1960s at Harvard, but Wilson and I were delighted when Harvard's President,

Nathan Pusey, and his MIT counterpart, James Killian, cut quickly through the barriers. Moynihan would direct the Center and teach two courses at the Education School, one a large lecture class about education and American cities and another a seminar on some aspect of education and urban politics. Moynihan accepted Harvard's offer.

Upon his arrival in early July 1966, Moynihan strode into my Harvard office, flung a pile of paper on my desk, and announced, in the colorful manner with which I quickly became accustomed, "This is the most dangerous report in the history of American education. What, Mr. Dean, are you going to do about it?" The report had an innocent-seeming title, a report to the Congress on "equal educational opportunity." It was, I soon learned, the second largest social science survey in history. A team led by the University of Chicago sociologist James S. Coleman had conducted it.

I had been a Dean long enough by then to know how to parry such a gambit. "No, Mr. Professor, what are *you* going to do about it?" (Whatever *it* is.)

And so, spurring one another along, in just a few months a grant from the Carnegie Corporation had been secured and Moynihan and a score of Harvard and kindred colleagues from beyond our campus set about re-running on the university computers the data gathered by Coleman and subjecting those findings to the scrutiny of a sustained seminar of experts drawn from a variety of quarters.

The report had been mandated in Section 402 of the Civil Rights Act of 1964, which instructed the United States Commissioner of Education to "conduct a survey and make a report to the President and the Congress . . . concerning the lack of availability of equal educational opportunities for individuals by reason of race, color, religion, or national origin in public educational institutions at all levels."[4]

The Congress had not specified just what it meant by "equal educational opportunity." Commissioner Francis Keppel filled this vacuum not by coming up with a description but by gathering a remarkable team of scholars led by Coleman, a team whose first task was to fashion a persuasive definition stark enough to lend itself to measurement and adaptable enough to affect policy. Traditionally, as both Coleman and Moynihan knew, educational "equality" had been defined by "inputs," meaning the quality of school buildings, the size of classes, the opportunities for extracurricular opportunities and such. Coleman and his colleagues put this definition on its head. Equal opportunity was to be measured by "outputs," for this study scores arising from tests of 570,000 schoolchildren. If students from various differing groups scored roughly the same, then there was one sort of "equality." If they did not, what might that tell us both about those children and about American educational policy?

It was this "output" rather than "input" matter that caused Moynihan to term the Equal Educational Opportunity Report "dangerous": it forced Americans to see their schools differently from the manner to which they had become accustomed. Effectiveness lay not in what a community *offered* as school but in what the students *displayed* as a result of attending the school that mattered. In a profound way, the Coleman team invented what drove the efforts of the so-called standards movement in the 1990s.

Moynihan and his colleague Frederick Mosteller, a Harvard mathematician and statistician, were quick to identify both the genius of this "output" decision as well as its significant shortcomings. "At the same time that we emphasize the importance of outputs," they wrote in 1972, in a volume edited by Moynihan and Mosteller arising from the seminar's work, "the reader [of the Equal Educational Opportunity Report] must take note that academic achievement is but one output, and that schooling is expected to produce many others. Retention rates, proportion going to college, income and occupation of graduates, even happiness, are a few of the outputs that might be measured." They also reminded the reader that "studies [based on test scores] do *not* find adult social achievement well predicted by academic achievement."[5] They acknowledged a "fundamental conflict" embedded in the work: the 1964 Civil Rights Act "*outlawed* group identification," but Coleman's research had to acknowledge groups' identities to plumb the possibility of "equality."[6]

Moynihan, joined by Thomas Pettigrew, an Associate Professor of Social Relations in the Faculty of Arts and Sciences, Mosteller, and ultimately almost eighty colleagues drawn from Harvard, other universities, government, and the foundations, made up a "Seminar" that met regularly, largely around a core group with much coming and going, for regularly scheduled dinners and debates at the Harvard Faculty Club. Grist for these sessions came from a variety of quarters, including a core staff led by several graduate students at the School of Education who were restudying Coleman's data and staffing several small group inquiries. The result was the volume edited by Moynihan and Mosteller, which included essays arising from and reanalyzing the data collected by Coleman and his group.

For me, the Seminar was frequently bewildering. An English major in college with a Ph.D. devoted largely to educational history and a military and schoolteaching career behind me, I was befogged and frequently cowed by the ferocious arguments within the Seminar about what struck me as dazzling but sometimes picayune statistical acrobatics, about the weight of different sorts of evidence, and about just what the humming new IBM computers at Harvard could and could not do with the thousands of Coleman's punched cards. Less puzzling for me were the discussions that arose from analyses, whether or not every seminarian agreed with the technical rigor of each. To my historian's and schoolteacher's eye, Moynihan and Mosteller's conclusions rang as authentic.

Moynihan and Mosteller quoted Coleman's troubling finding that the older the student—that is, the longer he or she had been in school—the wider the achievement gap between rich and poor became. There were few school-to-school variations. What mattered was social class. "The sources of educational opportunity appear to lie first in the home itself and the cultural influences immediately surrounding the home," Coleman wrote. "Then they lie in the schools' ineffectiveness to free achievement from the impact of the home and in the schools' cultural homogeneity which perpetuates the social influences of the home and its environs."[7] Moynihan and Mosteller summarized: the Equal Educational Opportunity Report "found that schools receive children who already differ widely in their levels of educational achievement. The schools thereafter do not close the gaps between students aggregated into ethnic/racial groups. Things end much as they begin." They quickly tempered that blunt assessment: "To the simple of mind or heart, such findings might be interpreted to mean that 'schools don't make any difference.' This is absurd. Schools make a very big difference to children. Children don't make up algebra on their own."[8]

This stung me personally. The "finding" that a child's achievement is not likely to be changed much by the size of her class, the quality of her teachers, and the seriousness of purpose of her school struck me as both misleading and unpersuasively deterministic. Nonetheless, the data, crude though they might be, sat there. They did not say that we teachers were utterly incompetent in what we were doing. They said that there was perhaps much, much more to children's learning than what existing schools, even at their best, might do.

Although the Study started with a focus on race and ethnicity rather than social class, Moynihan and Mosteller pointed out that the "presence of social class was implicit in the stated finding that family background, measured in social class terms—primarily education of parents, but including many other considerations such as the presence of an encyclopedia in the home—is apparently a major determinant of educational achievement."[9] This reminded me at the time of a cynical saw about "good" schools that I had repeatedly heard in the 1950s: *Let me pick the students' parents and I will show you a successful school.* I kept that gloomy maxim to myself; the data-drenched seminar was likely to be impatient with the easy gossip of an ex-schoolteacher.

More emerged from Moynihan and Mosteller: "The higher the social class of the other students the higher any given student's achievement." Again, an old saw from the 1950s: *Give me a solid corps of com-*

mitted kids in class and they will drag most of the others along. My military experience was, I felt, germane here. Many of the young soldiers with whom I had trained came from homes with low incomes and from schools in those communities, schools that fit the Coleman definition of "low performing." The demanding and starkly confined regimen of the peacetime but on-war-footing mid-1950s Army, led by confident veterans, pushed them hard. Many responded quickly, and, with the G.I. Bill to support formal education when they had completed their tour of duty, many surely eventually joined the middle class.

As the Seminar's discussions evolved, the debates among the participants bubbled. Ideology got tangled on data. Indeed, the data collected were themselves an expression of ideology, the choice of items to be considered itself a point of view. The Seminar supported inquiries that grew out of these confrontations, and ultimately no one was surprised that its final report—Moynihan and Mosteller's book—was a collection of papers, some disputing others. The genius of the effort was, however, that everyone's argument started with the same frame of reference, a large collection of data.

If "class" counts, what is "class"? Another Harvard colleague, Edward C. Banfield of the Government Department, had a novel definition, one that appeared to him to explain something important about contemporary metropolitan growth in America. Writing in his 1968 book *The Unheavenly City: The Nature and the Future of Our Urban Crisis,* Banfield showed how some families—rich or poor in economic terms—moved away from troubled communities, usually inner-city slums, to less-troubled, more cohesive communities, usually on a city's rim or in the suburbs. These people acted on the basis of aspirations for their family's years ahead. As Banfield described them, they were future oriented. He clearly admired them and wished that their numbers would increase.

Banfield created a crude typology to describe social classes, one different from that of grouping by income level. An upper-class individual, he wrote, "expects a long life, looks forward to the future of his children, grandchildren, and great-grandchildren, and is concerned also for the future of such abstract entities as the community, nation, or mankind." Banfield summarized: "He is confident that . . . he can, if he exerts himself to do so, shape the future." The middle-class person "plans ahead for his children and perhaps his grandchildren" but his time horizon and aspirations are more limited than his counterpart in the upper class. The working-class individual invests even less heavily in the future as does a middle-class person. "He has less confidence than the middle-class individual in his ability to shape the future and has a stronger sense of being at the mercy of fate." The lower-class person "lives from moment to moment."[10]

Banfield knew that this characterization would cause him grief in many circles. He opened his preface with a caveat. "This book will probably strike many readers as the work of an ill-tempered and mean-spirited fellow. I would not mind that especially if I did not think that it might prevent them from taking its argument as seriously as they should. I should like to assure the reader that I am as well meaning—probably even as softhearted—as he. But facts are facts, however unpleasant."[11]

As a person interested in schooling, I found Banfield's typology usefully provocative. A student, from whatever economic class, with a strong "future orientation" was one who would dig into the work I assigned him. He would accept my claim that if he worked hard at what I assigned him today he would be more adept at our shared interests tomorrow. He would put aside any expectation of immediate gratification. Pushing the argument further, I thought, one goal of schooling might be to encourage such striving, and that at the least a student who did not "do well" (that is, was dismissed as "stupid") might be thought to lack motivation rather than a lack of "smarts." A successful school might be best described as one that produced "upper-class"—future-oriented—graduates.

As a college teacher, I also learned how constructively upsetting Banfield's argument was with undergraduate and graduate students. Most believed passionately that Banfield, as he predicted, was indeed a very "mean-spirited fellow." Much though they did not like it, however, the students could not escape a belief in the general dictum, *Give me a youngster who wants to learn and in time I will show you a succeeder.* The aphorism works better the other way, *Give me a youngster who does not want to learn, who sees no point in learning the abstractions and skills that I am pressing upon him, and I will show you a failure,* that is, a failure in an educator's terms. However defined, Banfield's typology kept the college students and nascent professional educators very awake and usually frustrated as they found themselves ultimately arguing with themselves: they wanted to teach kids specific matters that they themselves valued, they were loath to define their roles as altering their students' visions of their futures, and they were uneasy with "labeling" people on evidence less certain than family income.

In the Seminar I was reminded that the line between opinion and fact is in all likelihood a fuzzy one, and that any particular collection of "data" that purports to "show" or even to "prove" something must be handled with the greatest of care. The reasonable, highly informed people in the Seminar could and did persuasively disagree over Coleman's data. Moynihan's description of the Coleman research as "dangerous" was entirely apt. The wisest of authorities are almost always, to me at least, the reserved ones. They know well and respect the fragility of the particular ground on which they stand.

Coleman's findings of the importance of class as a predictor of academic achievement reinforced for me the ideas expressed by Bailyn about an earlier American time. Education arises from a welter of influences, not just schools and indeed perhaps especially not schools, given how ineffectively they are currently designed. What counts is with whom a young person consorts and what images invade his world.

Cloisters

In the early 1980s, my wife, Nancy, and I spent a day visiting a Roman Catholic boarding school for girls on the West Coast. The school, set in rolling and, given recent rains, explosively green hills, served a few hundred young women largely within an enclosed campus, a place of palpable calm and order. The students came disproportionately from wealthy families, many from South America. The faculty comprised a mix of Sisters and laywomen. The kids were welcoming, easy with us, and, while predictably restless adolescents, notably positive about their school, something that the two of us (given our ill-informed prejudices about excessively cloistered schools) did not expect. Their routines were regulated, gently but firmly, we inferred, over each day's every hour. There was plenty of laughter but little of it that we heard was cutting or raucous. We visited good classes, in particular a memorable one in English taught by an elderly, almost other-worldly Sister.[12] By its very functioning, the school bore witness to principled, thoughtful order, albeit one that was not the world to which these young women would soon enter.

To a remarkable degree, this school deliberately and explicitly controlled with whom the students consorted and what images surrounded them. The staff and the Order that they represented believed that the world should not crash abruptly around children's heads (and souls) and that caring adults should moderate the process of enculturation. From gradually and systematically learning how to get along in a complex culture, the young women would, by their late teens, be strong in coping with harsh realities. Let them learn to swim in warm-water pools tended by lifeguards, the school believed, rather than hurl them early and unprotected into a cold and crashing surf. Fewer will drown, and all will eventually head into the waves as strong as possible. In the case of this Catholic school, the setting was almost entirely contrived, in a deliberate and benevolent sense. It was no surprise to me that one of James Coleman's later research projects focused in part on Catholic schools.

Although this school in its cloistered character was far distant from the schools that gathered the "equal educational opportunity" research interest of James Coleman, Pat Moynihan, and Edward Banfield, its functioning reflected much of what they had identified as crucial in the enculturation of and learning by adolescents. The classrooms are part of it, but the *surround* of those classrooms is crucial.

While I served as Headmaster of Phillips Academy at Andover during the 1970s, we explored ways and means by which this sturdy, well-endowed secondary boarding school—itself a contrived "surround," one which some call an academic pressure cooker—might provide a powerful educational experience that was *complementary* to (not a replacement for) that which a young person was experiencing at home and in his or her local high school. "Boarding" is expensive, but might a full-time, total immersion—a ten-week, twenty-four-hours-a-day focus, say on learning Russian—that was an adjunct to a youngster's "regular" high school enrollment be useful? Jerry Foster, an English teacher, and some of his colleagues pushed the issue from a practical standpoint: what could Andover offer for $1,000 per student, a sum that was readily "raise-able," with the sustained help of Andover alumni, in most communities?

The first result was the Andover Short-Term Institutes: sun-up-to-well-after-dark immersion in German or Russian, in Art, in Astronomy (with sleep during the day, all night spent with the telescopes), and other fields, scheduled for up to ten weeks during the academic year. That is, the students and faculty were wholly engaged in one "subject," under the best possible circumstances.

Another, more traditional approach was to increase the numbers of one- and two-year students, thereby "complementing" their first two or three years of high school. This approach had the further virtue of spreading the Academy's financial aid across more worthy adolescents than was possible with a student body composed of four-year enrollees: the argument here was the greatest good for the greatest number, quality being constant, maturity rather than chronological age being relevant, and variety of background being a virtue.

A focused addition to the Summer Session followed, this one for students of color—a program named (ms)2, mathematics and science for minority students—which offered intensive, interwoven work in mathematics, science, and English language over three summers for students drawn from a collaborating group of city and Native American Reservation public high schools.

For practical reasons (some of them attitudinal: going to two schools at a time is a substantial leap for a teenager), the winter session STIs did not survive. One- and two-year students are routinely admitted to the Academy. The program (ms)2 thrives to this day, with close connections forged between the Academy and a group of remarkable schools across the country that serve economically needy children.

Transitions to Adulthood

During the 1970s and thereafter, scholarly interest in the dimensions of this "surround of schools" continued. Coleman led another study, this time for President Nixon's Science Advisory Committee, entitled *Youth: Transition to Adulthood*.[13] There he presciently identified the information-rich culture with which early twenty-first century adolescents are surrounded, and he urged policy makers to ponder both its powerful influence and the implications for the design of school systems. "School is not a complete environment," he summarized. Lamentably, few paid much attention.

Further research and analyses on this and kindred matters followed from such scholars as Milbrey McLaughlin, Lisbeth Schorr, Laurence Steinberg, Mihalyi Csikszentmihalyi, Barbara Schneider, and others.[14] All illumined the inevitable and powerful interactions of school and all that lay beyond school in the lives of adolescents. Steinberg put it starkly in 1996: "Our findings suggest that the sorry state of American student achievement is due more to the conditions of students' lives outside of schools than it is to what takes place within school walls. In my view, the failure of the school reform movement to reverse the decline in achievement is due to its emphasis on reforming schools and classrooms, and its general disregard of the contributing forces that, while outside the boundaries of the school, are probably more influential."[15]

Most recently, Robert Putnam, in his book *Bowling Alone: The Collapse and Revival of American Community*, pulled together much previous research relating to social networks and organizations in the lives of citizens that documents their importance. "A state's social infrastructure is far more important than anyone would have predicted in ensuring the healthy development of youth. . . . The Social Capital Index [Putnam's metric for the existence and strength of community formal and informal organizations] is highly correlated with student scores on standardized tests taken in elementary school, junior high, and high school, as well with the rate at which students stay in school. . . . The correlation between community infrastructure, on the one hand, and student and parental engagement in schools, on the other hand, is very substantial even after taking into account other economic, social, and educational factors." Putnam cites Coleman as urging us not to underestimate "the importance of the embeddedness of young persons in the enclaves of adults most proximate to them, first and most prominently the family and second, a surrounding community of adults."[16]

Once again, even in the face of this barrage of carefully analyzed data, silence reigned in the education policy community. Putnam and his army of research assistants had done the hard work of collecting and analyzing a wide array of studies. His argument made scholarly sense and rang true to professionals in the field. Its impact on education policy, however, has been imperceptible.

My hunch is that this is not by chance. Policy makers (or more likely their staffs) read serious work by scholars like Putnam. However, the policy implications of these findings are so necessarily startling, so challenging to status quo thinking, inevitably so disruptive of the systems already "in place," that they must be quickly put out of mind.

Leadership?

Late in 2002 I had a long telephone call with an old friend that was devoted largely to the details of what each of us was doing "in retirement." A trustee of a major university and a counselor to a major graduate school of education, he was deeply involved in advising the presidents of both institutions. In both cases he was recommending programs in "leadership" for recruits to the cause of urban education. He felt that such initiatives were of obvious, pressing importance.

"Why just urban education?" I asked.

"That's where the problem rests," he replied. "Everyone agrees with that."

I confessed that I did not agree, believing the problem to be both broader and deeper. I took another tack.

"Leadership, yes: but *in what direction?*" I asked.

After a pause, he slipped over that question, implying that, for him at least, its answer was self-evident. If there were smart, devoted people at the helm, if they understood how to motivate people, if they collected "data" and acted on them, all, in time, would be well. By implication the educational vessel was aptly designed; it just needed decisive steering.

The contrary facts so powerfully illumined by James Coleman and a score of other scholars appeared to have barely touched the education systems' most powerful advocates. For them school remains a building within a system. Leaders are to run those schools well and superintend that system. Give those leaders ways and means of inspiration and a vocabulary of generalized tricks ("change must be data driven"), tell them they are the saviors of America's children, and go no further. Above all, they are not to challenge the core of ideas embraced by the system and its leaders (whatever the unsettling data from such people as James Coleman might suggest).

I blathered on about all that, with my mind filled with grotesque images of First World War infantry charges led by Sandhurst-trained, peach-fuzz-cheeked British lieutenants into the hail of German ma-chine-gun fire. Suicide it was; if experience were to be respected, such an assault had only a small chance of success, much less of survival of the lieutenants in the lead. It took months of slaughter to suggest to some maverick young political leaders in London that there had to be a better way to crack the German lines.

Even though I kept these macabre images to myself—of bright young school system "leaders" hurled wave upon wave into a demonstrably dysfunctional system—my friend from the telephone call surely found my tone a tad naive and a bit more than a tad self-righteous. He was probably right on both counts.

Configurations

Nonetheless, no practicing educator that I know ever would say that what happens outside of school does not affect how a student behaves within school. Few such educators that I know, however, move much beyond this truism. They acknowledge it but almost always turn abruptly back to the immediate world of their particular schools, the classes assigned, the moneys allotted, the assessments imposed, the professionals' routines categorized, the schedules promulgated, each in exquisite detail.

When confronted with this charge, most say that no one can take on the whole world at once. At least, they argue, we professional edu-cators have the children in school. They present plenty enough chal-lenge in our classrooms. Let us focus there.

I understand this. It is a practical reaction. Given the enormous play of influences on young people, especially adolescents, any other reaction could be read as silly, unlikely to lead anywhere useful and might diminish what we can do at school.

Unfortunately, however, multiple influences sap the impact of any one influence, be it family or school. If they want stable and believable results, realistic policy makers and on-the-line educators associated with them must tackle more than one influence simultaneously, "silly" though at first it may appear. Indeed, they have no choice. Images and opportunities from all quarters bombard children whether school people want it or not. What students learn from all this bombardment is as unclear as it is likely to be substantial.

The historian Lawrence A. Cremin called such weaving of influences on a young citizen's learning "configurations of education." In his 1976 collection of essays in honor of John Dewey entitled simply *Public Education*, he described a "fundamental problem" as "the tendency to focus so exclusively on the potentialities of the school as a lever of social improvement and reform as to ignore the possibilities of other educative institutions."[17] He spoke of a "century-long over-reliance on schooling as a general instrument of social aspiration to a widespread disenchantment with schooling."[18]

Cremin went on: "Given an awareness of the multiplicity of institutions that educate, one soon perceives the tendency of such institutions at particular times and places to relate to one another in what might be called configurations of education. Each of the institutions within a configuration interacts with the others and with the larger society that sustains it and that is in turn affected by it. Configurations of education also interact, as configurations, with the society of which they are a part."[19] The education of each child emerges from the interplay, or lack of interplay, of the various elements within the configuration.

Cremin points out that "in the ordinary course of living, education is *incidental;* in schooling it is *intentional.*"[20] However, the jobs that Mr. Sleepy and his classmates at the city school I visited needed for money were not merely "incidental." They were intentional, in that their families depended on them. Mr. Sleepy may be exceptional in the heaviness of the job load he carried, but he was hardly unique. School is not the only intentional institution in adolescents' lives.

Further, Mr. Sleepy and his agemates are subject to an unrelenting, inexpensive, ever accessible beat of sound, stories, and images from the media, many of great sophistication and measurable effect. Todd

Gitlin calls it "supersaturation." "In 1999," he wrote, "a television set was on in the average American household more than seven hours a day, a figure that has remained fairly steady since 1983. . . . Sex, race, income, age, and marital status make surprisingly little difference in time spent. . . . The Internet [has not] diminished total media use, even if you do not count the Web as part of the media. . . . The Internet redistributes the flow of unlimited media but does not dry it up. When one considers the overlapping and additional hours of exposure to radio, magazines, newspapers, compact discs, movies . . . and comic books . . . it is clear that the media flow into the home—not to mention outside—has swelled to a torrent of immense force and constancy, an accompaniment *to* life that has become a central experience *of* life. . . . Ninety-nine percent of children (age two through eighteen) live in homes with one or more TVs, 97 percent with a VCR, 97 percent with a radio, 94 percent with a tape player, 90 percent with a CD player, 70 percent with a video game player, 69 percent with a computer."[21]

The young people cannot avoid these forces any more than can their elders; indeed, many teenagers do not want to hide, as they find the allure of the media exciting, "grown up," and engaging, far more engaging than classes in drab, underfinanced schools. Virtually all of the media intrusion is attached to commerce. Much of it is advertising, and advertising, if not by definition then by demonstrable practice, marches at the edges of deceit, teaching a dubious moral message. The worldly configurations within which an American teenager lives are an excitement, alluring in their manipulation, thereby serving as both a boon and a threat.

There is, of course, enormous promise in this accessible technology including what is now called "online distance learning," thereby lessening the need for a building to house the students and their teachers and going directly to each student's academic work at "virtual" courses on his or her computer. All this is in its infancy, affecting so far only those children who have access to technology, the ability to master its operation, and the persistence to do so. Although professionals are skeptical, and wisely so, there is promise, not of a replacement for gathering places called schools but of an extension of those places. At its best, distance learning is a positive expression of the technology blitz that affects every young American, an addition to traditional "homeschooling" and an extension of "school-schooling." At its oversold worst, it will further atomize and cheapen what a serious secondary education can and must be.[22]

For educators, this is an utterly new world. The matter for education planners is not just finding a common ground for family, neighborhood, work, and school. The matter is now family, neighborhood, work, school, *and* the enormously broadening and inevitably manipulative—and information-giving—world of the media.

Cremin's "configurations" observation must now move beyond description to prescription. Cremin's portrayal of modern society's multiplicity of sources for learning is accurate. Coleman's information-rich society is with us; none of this will go away—the power of the culture's incidental but persistent and powerful media, for good and ill, can only increase. Therefore, however reluctantly, educators should accept Cremin's challenge and move toward the design of modern ways to educate youth—a very rethinking of deliberate education, rethinking that includes but goes substantially beyond the good things that can happen in the familiar building.

Prescribing an education that addresses all the aspects of a child's life and deliberately connects formal school with its larger surround will require a grand leap of imagination. Indeed, the very way I describe the prospect—"connecting formal school with its surround" —is constricting in that my picture implies a "place" with satellites. That will no longer do. The traditional ways of perceiving adolescents' learning must be held in check, the governing metaphors and familiar practices diligently challenged, and no idea peremptorily dismissed because of its presumed impracticality or perceived ideological roots; and all must be addressed at once. There should be no convenient silence here behind which to hide.

With this perspective, several approaches appeal to me as a way to start. None is bizarre, though some already cause discomfort in many quarters. None is new. They spread across a wide ideological spectrum, from Ivan Illich to Milton Friedman, from the radical Left to the arch Right, from HomeSchool advocates to those who sell curricula that are intended to be taught to all in serried ranks. Most are employed today, in some limited, albeit often dysfunctional, form. When pushed hard, however, all force fresh thinking.

First, accept the inconvenient reality that no two children are ever quite the same. Although patterns occur in their development, there will never be one predictable regime that serves all children as well as each deserves. Further, accept the reality that some students need more support and protection from the state than others do, and that the shape of this support and protection, given individual needs, will vary.

Second, define mandatory education in terms of performance rather than school attendance. Define ultimate "performance" as more than the short-term regurgitation of matters "covered" in classes, and extend that "performance" to a student's demonstrated habit of the use of essential knowledge and skills in unfamiliar but realistic situations over time, all this assessed by various means. Develop more avenues for learning both within and beyond the schoolhouse, including the existing media channels.

Third, insist that all citizens equitably bear the real costs of this education.

Fourth, bundle public education funding of children and families with the finance for other programs serving the same people (like that for housing, physical and mental health, and job preparation) and arrange for these bundled moneys to be spent in ways promising the greatest effectiveness for the individuals and family units involved, thereby creating incentives for collaboration. Where appropriate, closely relate public and publicly supported institutions and programs with congenial efforts in the private sector, including churches. The end here is a web of relationships and services, public and private, that accommodate all youngsters, creating a variety of constructive communities that serve as social capital.

Fifth, arrange for the "sites" for this education to include existing institutions, such as homes, workplaces, the media, and the "street" as well as newly focused schools.

Sixth, have public funds follow the child rather than being funneled into the institutions, with more funds placed behind the children of poorer families than those of comfortable affluence. Require public inspection of places where that money can be spent. Let the parents, on a lottery basis, choose the educational arrangements for their child. Be alert to issues of civil rights: assure that the voices of the poor are heard and their legitimate needs are met.

Seventh, reenergize and reconfigure the 1965 initiative that led to public television, creating all-day child-friendly educational programming and Internet access that is not closely tied to commerce.[23] Extend to the greatest imaginative extent "distance learning." Tax the for-profit media sector fully to support this work.

Finally, tolerate variety in the expression of these ideas.

There is something on this list, I know, for everyone to hate and to love. Most of these items have an ideological history. When I raise them, the temptation of many is to go quickly and critically to practical details, usually choosing extreme situations. It is hard, I have learned, to present these suggestions as an interwoven package; there is an itch to pull the proposals apart. This hurts, as several depend on others. Most dismiss the package as too complicated.

All that said, no one has yet argued with me that children do not differ. Nonetheless, the temptation to slip into mechanical-age grading appears irresistible. We are too impatient, and we search for easy solutions to what we know are very complicated realities.

Many gag at the requirement of demonstrated performance replacing that of attendance. I remind them of state driver's tests, of adjudicated science fairs, of athletic contests, of Scouts' merit badges, of the "troubleshooting" competitions among vocational-technical school auto mechanics courses, of concerts, recitals, and art shows, of the exquisitely detailed work of admissions committees in competitive colleges, of moot court trials in law schools, of juried design projects in architectural schools. The list is endless. There can be far more to demonstration of performance than intellectually shriveling paper-and-pencil tests.

Many counter by pointing out that there are no crisp, singular "results" in most of these examples. Without authoritative-appearing, exquisite precision, they ask, how can we rank and rate students? Precise gradations are part of existing school culture—valedictorian, rank in class, and all that—and many believe that the system absolutely expects such precision. The fact that there is little scholarly evidence supporting the validity of the practice is steadfastly avoided (itself an irony). Nonetheless, the drum beats on. Who is Number One? There *has* to be a Number One! The insistence is silly; most understand that fact, but few articulate the understanding, much less figure out how to act upon it. A more general, generous, and respectful system seems out of reach.

Few quarrel with the expectation that all of us will pool our (tax) money to support all our children. Many quarrel, however, about just who "all our children" are (Our kids and our neighbors' kids in this town? All the kids in the state? All American kids?).

Those who have had experience with the disbursement of dollars for social and educational services are chary of "bundling," believing that it could create a bureaucratic nightmare and make possible a net decrease in funding. The well-organized lobbies for, say, children with special needs might be less ready to fight for adequate general funding (even as it includes special needs funding) than for continued targeted, protected funding.

Few appreciate the costly inefficiency of many current school facilities (and thus the financial waste)—they are used for their primary funded purpose for barely half the year—and worry about the lack of a "building" or a "campus." Most assume that all children will be in school at the same time. For many parents school is first and foremost a predictable babysitter at public expense.

Money following the child? Vouchers! Many recoil, seeing the practice as a "for-profit privatization" idea. The G.I. Bill of Rights for military veterans, hardly a sinister privatization gambit, was and is a voucher system. Most state's "choice" programs, including attendance at regional vocational schools, expect the dollars to follow the child. Special needs moneys follow the child. How money moves is a technical matter. To whom it may be directed is a political matter.

As to parental choice: I have known no family that did not absolutely desire and expect it. I know many families that have acted on that expectation, largely because they knew how to work the system and had the money and time to do it. I have known many families, most of them poor, that wanted it (or at least wanted more out of the school to which their child had been assigned) but were not in a position to demand it. "Choice" has become almost as volatile a word as "voucher." Again, given the school/school district–choosing behavior of wealthier Americans, I suspect that the word, like "voucher," has been hijacked for a political purpose (if you are rich, you can choose; if you are not rich, tough luck). To me, if most Americans want choices among schools for their children and if some (wealthier) Americans can act upon it, why not all Americans?

Directing policy attention away from school systems—school *buildings* as a metaphor—and on to the most effective education of children, wherever that takes place and whatever it requires, is a Herculean task. Until Americans understand the reality of the lives of Mr. Sleepy and his friends and act accordingly, they will continue to skirt the edges of a serious education, even as most go through the motions. Unless something is done about Mr. Sleepy's home, work, and school worlds *in combination*, and probably about the terror of his family's poverty, he will drift into a life with few, and likely limited, opportunities whatever energies his teachers might expend on his behalf.

I am surer of the responsibility to look at formal schooling as but a bit of what education is than I am of how precisely to act on what I see. I am painfully aware of the paucity of serious thinking—the *silence*—about what growing up American means, and even more so about the prospect of an America genuinely "formed" (as Bailyn put it) by our current arrangements for schooling.

It is not that we do not care. It is that we all are fearfully stuck in old metaphors, none more than that of an *orderly* school *system* embodied in *buildings*.

2 Authority

"You're The Man," I was told by a cheeky kid in our school, probably in a clumsy attempt to flatter me. No ambiguity, no silence here; or none that that young man could fathom.

As the Acting co-Principal of a four-year-old late twentieth-century public charter school, I did not feel like The Man, the In Charge, the Pedagogue on a White Horse, the Force, the Wise-and-Stern Dispenser of Punishments and Indulgences. Whatever. Nothing at all like that.

My co-Principal, who happened to be my wife, Nancy, might have been told that she was the Woman. But no (and assuming that this student would so address her in this way at all, which was unlikely): she would have been told that she too was The Man.

Truth be told, at this small new secondary school I felt as if we had only the flimsiest grasp of what was going on, much less being a two-person Man. Nancy and I had temporarily inherited a sturdy but pitching vessel carrying devotedly committed children, parents, and teachers that was being constructed while under sail. Issues rushed at us from every direction, a fair number of which were unexpected. State inspectors lurked. Doubting Thomases were in abundance. Unsure of what went and what didn't, some kids tested us daily. Others, mercifully, understood our predicament and were even fascinated by it. We called the eldest of them Senators and solicited their help, believing that we needed to gather to the cause every mind and heart engaged with us, especially those of our oldest, most mature students.[1]

From earlier experience, I knew that a principal's very partial hold on events was not unique to new schools. During the 1970s I had been the principal of what by American standards was a large and very well established school, Phillips Academy, two hundred years old. The traditional imagery there of the All-Powerful Headmaster to the contrary, I learned that while I was the ultimate helmsman, the ideas and mores that students, adults, and the mood of the times carried with them profoundly affected the direction of the vessel, whether I liked it or not. Much though I might have wished that I were The Man, able to leap over academic and bureaucratic squabbles, it was never possible. Nor, I learned, would it have been a wholly intelligent posture.

Nonetheless, many principals that I have met are attracted to this "The Man" characterization. They have been endlessly told that they are Leaders. They talk of "*my* school" as though they owned it and rarely in the sense of a family where at best they are first among equals. The metaphor of "possession" is ludicrous. I have come to call these folk *L'Ecole, C'est Moi* pedagogues, in the tradition attributed to Louis XIV of France. Books are written celebrating the inspirational teacher or the axe-handle-wielding principal or the stern but loving school head or the management-bedazzled follower of some organizational guru. Like most testimonials, these portraits are partly persuasive, partly myopic, and to a veteran like me largely unconvincing.

The hard fact is that, more than anyone else, students, by virtue of their numbers, drive high schools—albeit indirectly, obliquely, unintentionally, often by default. The adolescents typically outnumber adults fourteen to one. The faculty and staff outnumber principals from ten to one to several hundred to one. Thus to be a worthy helmsman in most circumstances is to be clear, visible, close to the important action, fair, and decisive—and to pray for an experienced crew, understanding parents, "nice" kids, gentle bosses, and good weather.

This characterization of schools and leadership both describes reality and suggests a way of looking at schools, especially secondary schools, which are places where the students are at once children and adults, dependent and independent, bursting with autonomy and hungry for adult affirmation and approval, confident-seeming, their talk more assured than honestly questing, but clearly scared about their futures. School keeping cannot be represented by a neat hierarchical chart of roles, with "power" at the top.

What concerns me is the extent of the *silence* about who exactly manages secondary schools. My experience is that successful schools "run" on the basis of a series of understandings among the engaged partners, some of whom are close in, some removed. A principal explicitly or implicitly makes "treaties" with these various estates: the school's teachers and staff, the school's students, the students' parents or guardians, the customs and pressures from sister schools in the district and region, the district's central office, the community within which the school sits, the unions (whether formally organized or clusters of people who have a tradition of being heard), the district's school board, state authorities, federal authorities, local customs and expectations, associations (such as athletic conferences), external pressure groups and lobbies, the press, the school's "reputation"—not to mention immediate crises, such as budget shortfalls.[2]

School leaders I admire are those who have created a constructive balance of authority in their particular situations. They make "treaties," many of them unspoken, with the various estates. Those treaties are very local; a successful principal may arrange her affairs quite differently from another comparably successful principal down the street. The treaties are not primarily accepting of the status quo. Rather, they are treaties reflecting the central priorities of the school's leader, those embedded in the realities of the local situation, adapted as situations change and pressures wax and wane.

Such "treaties" cannot be dismissed as nuisances. Rather, they are the stuff of democracy. Wise principals value them. Balanced authority —a crafting of shared responsibilities by means of "treaties"—is the heart of the American system.

The Nature of Authority

Authority is a loaded, complex term. Richard Sennett has pondered it. "The need for authority is basic. Children need authorities to guide and reassure them. Adults fulfill an essential part of themselves in being authorities; it is one way of expressing care for others." And yet Sennett reminds us that "we have come to fear the influence of authority as a threat to our liberties, in the family and in society at large. The very need for authority redoubles our modern fear: Will we give up our liberties, become abjectly dependent, because we want so much for someone to take care of us?"[3]

Sennett implies agreement with the paradox of compulsory education in a liberal democratic society: *We will force you to learn in order that you may become free.* Democracy is not about mindless obedience. Democracy depends on informed, imaginative, engaged, independent people who know when to act and when to show restraint.

"It is perfectly true that you cannot force people to do what might give them freedom," Sennett writes. What is required is persuasive engagement, younger with older, old with old, young with young. This engagement is, in fact, what we call democracy. "Interpretation of complex phenomena"—that is, the discussion of merits and the reaching of equitable conclusions—"takes up time, is inefficient, creates unhappiness and tension. These are well-worn arguments against the democratic process. It is simply a matter of facing the fact: if one really believes in democratic ideals and accepts the necessity of chains of command at the same time, these confrontations are necessary. They are not evasions."[4]

My observation and experience is that such engagement in a school has the paradoxical effect of increasing the power—the authority—of its leader. All of us are more likely to pull together if each of us has had a respectful role in the process: there must be a *balance* among us. However, an attenuated process can lead to stalemate and resentment. A wise leader senses the moment of paralysis when everyone has talked enough. Getting the best decision made, even roughly asserted, is necessary. How to accomplish this without losing authority is a tricky, often painful business.

Authority as Power

What makes public education special in America's democracy is the absolute requirement that citizens of a certain age attend schools and that governments raise the moneys to pay for those schools. That is, government commands and exacts obedience under penalty of the law. At the margins there are home schoolers and children in private schools, but these are partial exceptions to the means, not to the end. Americans *will* be schooled, each for at least twelve years, at public expense. No requirement within American democracy has a comparably universal claim. Given the extent of this claim, an argument for balanced, democratically managed authority makes as much sense system-wide as it does for the functioning of an individual school.

Put in skeletal form, that balance could take the following form:

The *state* (meaning state governments, where in America responsibility for schooling has historically resided) would raise the necessary capital and operating moneys from general taxation and affirm, by authorization of proposed designs and by inspection, the extent and functioning of public schools or gatherings of public schools, these gatherings being regional (as is the case now with school districts) or assembled by virtue of educational character (such as magnet schools that stress mathematics and science).

The *school*, or cluster of schools, would both design and provide formal education, on a single site or a grouping of sites, the design perhaps including formalized homeschooling and the use of such virtual or existing public resources as public libraries, educational Web sites, and community orchestras. The schools' designs and functioning would include an irreducible minimum of state-mandated forms and functions and would be subject to regular and rigorous inspection of their effectiveness against the commitments expressed in their state-approved design.

The *family*, or appointed guardians, would choose the school or schools that it wished its child to attend. Admission to that school would be by lottery, or, in special cases, by a controlled lottery (that is, places might be reserved for children from certain protected groups).

Authority thereby would be shared. The state would set the minimum standard, would provide finance (on relevant occasions with help from the Federal government), and would inspect on behalf of the People. The school would have both to meet the state's expectations and to earn the support of families. If few families wished to patronize a school, it would shut down. The family would have to make an affirmative choice and would thus be philosophically beholden to the program of that school.

What I have here described is already familiar in one form or another at the margins of most states. The notion here is new only to the extent that this system would become the rule rather than the exception, replacing the familiar top-down hierarchical bureaucracies that serve most American children.

Precedents like the arrangements for vocational and technical education and for various sorts of magnet schools are of long standing. The notion of individual public Charter schools has taken firm hold, and there are explorations of the possibilities and shape of Charter districts, schools gathered by educational character rather than geography.

An ambitious version of this realignment of authority was seen in the "Learning Zones" plan within the New York City schools, a proposal made in 1999 to the Annenberg Challenge, the extraordinary $500 million venture launched by Walter Annenberg for American school reform. Small, largely new public schools, each associated with one of four diverse organizations—New Visions, Acorn, the Manhattan Institute, and the Center for Collaborative Education—would be part of a largely self-governing group of their kindred schools, in whatever Borough they happened to be housed or at what level child —elementary, middle, or secondary—they served, and each group would collectively control substantial moneys that now flowed downward, along with requirements, from the larger bureaucracy. The then-Chancellor and Mayor approved, as did the then–New York State Commissioner of Education, the city's United Federation of Teachers, and a clutch of local foundations that agreed to match Ambassador Annenberg's grant two-for-one.

Within months, however, the Chancellor was forced out (an every-other-year practice over the past three decades in the city of New York) and a new Chancellor arrived, demanding his own agenda and brushing aside firm public commitments made by his predecessor. The Mayor stayed eerily silent, even as the moneys arriving from the foundations were taking a different path than originally intended. The Learning Zones persisted only by dint of political trench warfare and, when the external money ran out, largely disbanded, smothered by the familiar ways of an old order. Their "authority" was only as good as the word of the original political leaders. Unprotected by legislation or contract, they were easily blown away.

Clearly, the biggest danger in any shared authority arrangement is that the most powerful partner or partners will not act with restraint or consistency. The most potent partner in the skeletal plan that I suggest is usually state government, and the recent record of legislation and regulation at state level is not encouraging. The temptation of state authorities to overreach their mandates appears to have been irresistible.

By the end of the twentieth century, both education policy and practice in several states were being shaped in detail by small numbers of mostly appointed—not elected—bodies, often with a self-righteously ideological as well as political bent. Education has always been vulnerable to all sorts of fashions, but when a single fashion becomes lodged in ever higher levels of government, schooling itself is at risk. The idea that there might be several worthy "fashions" and multiple sets of equally worthy "standards and assessments," any one of which is likely to serve committed families well, has become unpopular.

L'Ecole, C'est Moi behavior appears increasingly to appeal to the top of the public school hierarchy.

Authority from Scholarship

"What did I get on the test?" one of my students asks.

"You got a 74."

She cavils. "A 74? Come on, I really knew that stuff." And perhaps she did, and I missed something. Or perhaps I had set a misleading question. Or perhaps she is bluffing or mistaken. Whether she deserved a 74 or not or whether her complaint is reasonable are matters testing my judgment. Indeed, what is a "74," save, in most cases, a vague abstraction?

Difficult as it is to grapple with questions as primordial as what a "74" might be, I-her-teacher cannot escape the responsibility of being an authority on each of my students. Without assessing what and why a student "knows," I cannot understand where her learning is, "know" being a broadly defined word. If I do not know what she "knows," I cannot teach her well. I must be an *authority* on each of my students, one by one. And to be such an authority I have to know deeply the area of study with which my student engages: the connection between her and the discipline is the name of school's game.

What does it take to be such an authority? I learned the answer from a master, albeit one who worked far from a high school classroom. My father, a professor of the history of art at Yale University, was an expert on the life and work of John Trumbull, the Revolutionary period American patriot and artist, best known for his heroic scenes that ring the wall of the Capitol's rotunda in Washington. When my father said, on the basis of his analysis, that a portrait had been painted by Trumbull, the museum and art collector's world absolutely accepted it. Dad's judgments were "high-stakes" judgments. A Trumbull may be worth many times what a picture might bring if it were the work of a lesser known artist or a forger, of which there were many in Trumbull's time. On such matters, Dad was the ultimate authority. His Trumbull "Check List" was the last word.[5]

One summer day in the early 1950s Dad invited me, an awkward teenager, to go with him to call upon an elderly woman who believed that she owned a portrait by Trumbull. As I recall it, Dad had already corresponded with her and received photographs of the oil painting. He believed that there was a sufficient chance that she was correct to justify a special trip. We drove to a small, old Connecticut town, one of those tranquil places centered around a village green on which sat an eighteenth-century white-steepled Congregational church, a setting that would have been familiar to Trumbull himself.

The lady welcomed us expectantly and led us to the portrait that hung over the fireplace. A formal tea had been set out. Dad looked carefully at the work. We all were silent. He gave no indication of his judgment, and he turned his formal but winning charm on our hostess. The teatime talk between the two was largely about genealogy, most particularly of the lady's family and of how the portrait had found its way into her parlor.

In time we departed, with no judgment expressed by Dad, a fact that must have disappointed our hostess. On the drive back, Dad remained quite still, obviously in thought. I recall my hunch by the time we reached our home in Bethany that he probably believed this portrait to be a fake, or a copy, or some sort of rogue painting—but not a Trumbull. Dad did not share his suspicions with me, or probably anyone else, until he had done more study, perhaps that which he drew from the talk with the lady about her forebears. If the painting was not by Trumbull, it still might have been by a notable, if lesser, artist.

Dad would advise her about that. His method, his restraint, and his courtesy fascinated me.

Most of Dad's evidence rested on a documentary record for each piece of art—the painter's notes, bills of sale, letters including transfers, and more. When such evidence was not available or was unconvincing, he turned to the works themselves—their canvas, their backing and framing, the quality of the paint, the brushwork, ultimately the style. Dates and places were important. "The matter of getting artist and sitter together (in which forgers often lamentably fail) has been arduous."[6] Naturally, if painter and subject were never in the same place for the requisite minimum of time, the hunch that the work was counterfeit was very strong. Dad traveled far beyond little Connecticut villages to see for himself what were claimed to be Trumbulls and necessarily dipped into English sources, as the painter had been trained in London.

When the documentary and physical record was insufficient, he turned to his personal judgment, including that arising from knowledge of Trumbull's painting technique. Of the "Check List" he wrote that "most of the attributions can be documented, and dates and places of execution verified; some, however, cannot, and attributions are based on stylistic evidence alone. In some instances pictures which I have been unable to see or study, or concerning which I have reservations, have been included with an interrogation mark in parentheses directly after the subject. . . . I wish to emphasize that attributions unsupported by documentary evidence, as well as omission of hundreds of paintings and drawings which I believe are erroneously ascribed to the artist, represent only my personal—and fallible—opinion."[7]

Dad was an excruciatingly careful scholar who looked at every sort of relevant evidence before making a final, firm judgment. When he had doubts he expressed them without embarrassment, signaling such with an "interrogation mark." He was so sure of himself that he could —indeed felt he must—mention that he was less than sure. This humility lay at the base of his authority.

Although utterly different in many obvious ways, growing children and two-hundred-year-old paintings are alike in their complexity. Paintings, however, stand still. Children do not. Becoming an authority on a painting requires varied, informed, and careful analysis. Being an authority on a child—even something as trivial as assigning a "74" to her paper—requires varied, informed, and careful analysis, over time. A teacher must know well both the child and the subject with which the child is struggling. Identifying paintings and the qualities of a child's work both require humility, as an absolutely sure diagnosis is rare.

Becoming an "authority" about a child is a demanding craft, infinitely more demanding than conventional public school policy and practice implies. Every thoughtful teacher therefore yearns to hear the sorts of cautions about children that Dad expressed about Trumbull's real and supposed works, especially when the stakes are high. An end to rigid pigeonholing of children on the basis of their ages alone would be a happy place to start. Finding an "interrogation mark" next to a student's score on a consequential standardized test would be nice. It would tell us that the examiners in this particular case, after careful consideration, were still uncertain. How thoughtful. How humble. How fair. How sophisticated. How quaint. How inconceivable in today's impatient and arrogant political climate.

The *silence* about this issue is as embarrassing as it is understandable. For a school to take children one by one would require either a sharp focusing of existing programs (thus reducing the student to teacher ratio within the surviving classes) or much more money, either or both requiring extraordinary political muscle.

Money is relevant. Rich people, by means of private schools or heavily funded public schools, pay knowledgeably and dearly to make sure that their children are known well and taught accordingly. Arthur G. Powell has written powerfully of this in his *Lessons from Privilege: The American Prep School Tradition*, a study of independent secondary schools.[8] Because these institutions are schools-of-choice and because the parents are the primary source of each school's income (or comparably within the public sector, with suburban or city magnet school parents who have substantial political clout), these places must respond to what families desire, and the evidence is, Powell argues, that they want "personalization." Those who pay tuitions know that "personal attention within small scale environments is a potent educational method. . . . Knowing the kids well is not sentimentality . . . but a tool to entice students into greater academic engagement than would otherwise not have occurred. . . . The most important prep school method of personalization is simply the attitude that it should permeate all aspects of school life. Every student (and teacher) is assumed to be worthy of both respect and special attention. . . . The average load of about sixty students per teacher in independent high schools"—as compared with 100 to 175 in many public senior high schools—"is one of the most telling statistics in American education."[9]

Authority as Character

A third definition of authority applies to *individual* behavior, where "authority" represents the power of one to influence others on the basis of their confidence in his or her judgment. This is exhibited authority, often subtle and oblique, difficult to define, even more difficult to train for but manifest in everyone's life. Most of us like being around people who demonstrably know what they are doing, who don't lose their cool unnecessarily, who are resourceful in coping with the unfamiliar.

This sort of authority arises both from personality and from experience. While hard to characterize, we know it when we see it. Teenagers spot such authoritative people quickly and either gravitate to them or, if they have something to hide, deliberately avoid them. Schools that have them in some numbers are blessed.

In 1964, when I became Dean of the Harvard Graduate School of Education, I had almost no experience with big city schools, save what I had gathered vicariously by reading in the library stacks. Accordingly,

I quickly set out on some visits, drawing on friendships with recent alumni. Mark Shedd, then the relatively new superintendent of the Philadelphia Public Schools, was one of them, and he was happy to open some doors, particularly that of West Philadelphia High School, whose students had garnered recent notoriety as participants in a ruckus—some called it a riot—with the city police. The students at West Philly, as they termed their school, were largely African American. Most were part of families struggling with low incomes. The principal welcomed me and assigned as my guide a young white administrator. I remember him as Phil.

The school building was raffish, and students wandered the halls at all times. I was turned over by Phil to a group of older kids, largely males, whom he deemed to be some of the leaders of the student body; they had been high-visibility actors in the police ruckus and the newspaper stories that reported it. Their spokesman was a wonderfully quick and good-humored young man named Eddie. He seemed delighted to bring the nervous white guy in the sober suit into the real world of West Philly High.

Eddie and his group led me on a tour of the school, chatting with me and, all along, with classmates in the hallways, some of whom appeared just to be roaming around, others sitting in groups on the floor. I had been warned that the place was very overcrowded and the rosters of just who should be here and who should not be there were out of date and incomplete. The tone of these noisy corridors was spirited but rarely menacing. We must have appeared to be a strange entourage. The stares unsettled me.

Eddie and his friends rhetorically pounded on the school, the school system, the police, the mayor, everyone in traditional authority. Their lack of respect was as full of wry humor as condemnation. Much of the cheerfully delivered invective turned on race.

What gradually struck me was that Phil was exempt from these tirades. He kept appearing in the stories as a fair-minded person who understood that which begged for understanding. At the end of the building tour, the group, save Eddie, scattered. I asked him why Phil seemed free from criticism even though he was a white administrator. Eddie quickly answered. "He's not white. He's black."

The answer was a metaphor, of course, and one reflecting a mid-1960s northern city setting and the workings on young minds of Martin Luther King Jr.'s message rather than the angrier views that emerged as the decade progressed. Nonetheless it has stuck with me. Something about Phil transcended race. He was, in a way, The Man for Eddie and his friends. He had authority, not so much organizational authority, not the ability to rule, but enough standing with the students to keep that place orderly for some, safe for most, and special for a group of adolescents who were, elsewhere, seething with rage and ready to express it.

What was that authority? I never knew Phil well enough to know for certain. I have hunches, however. He told the truth to everyone in any setting. This gained him the respect not only of the students but also of the superintendent. He was easy, good-natured, open, seemingly without fear or guile, but he clearly was no doormat. He moved in on kids who were out of order, risking thereby an embarrassing confrontation in the presence of a visitor. The students knew that he was a Grown-Up, not just an older guy who wanted to be one of the boys. He knew everybody, or faked it well. He could tell in an instant who were the kids who were not supposed to be in the building. I asked him how he knew. "By how they look at me."

Although the problems at West Philadelphia High School in 1964 extended far beyond the reach of a single school administrator, Phil kept the peace, pushed for what learning could then take place, and all the time retained the respect and even affection of a large student body, portions of which were close to explosion.

Was it a matter of personality? Yes, in part. He was confident. He genuinely liked adolescents, and they saw him as a person who could get good things done. He was not hung up on matters of prestige; he was not called "Doctor Jones" or its relevant equivalent. Just "Mister," like his faculty and staff peers. But not just a nickname like his students.

Was it something he had learned somewhere? Perhaps, in part. He knew what the ecology of a big city school might be and thus could manage it. Such knowledge rarely arises out of common sense alone.

Phil was around his school, not locked in an office behind a counter or in a conference room "downtown." He was visible to his flock and comfortable with them. He was a person, not an office. This struck me as a paradox. He used only lightly his systemic Authority to gain *authority*.

I talked later with Mark Shedd about the day. The superintendent knew that even a Phil could accomplish little more than to see to the schooling of some students really well, given the chaos and under-funding in the city's schools. At least the kids kept coming. There was hope in that. Shedd knew he was blessed with colleagues like Phil. What they could do was done, and then some.

Over the subsequent thirty years I have met many school people who had that fragile but powerful quality of personal authority. I have visited the schools of many of them and can quickly sense its power, whether within a single classroom or, as with Phil, in a school writ large. Sometimes you do not have actually to watch such a person in action in a school. If you know what to look for, you can sense it anywhere.

So it was for me with Michele Forman, the 2001 National Teacher of the Year and a 1967 graduate of Brandeis University, as she opened her remarks to an audience of faculty and students at her alma mater, in the spring of 2002. Forman was at the university to receive the Levi-tan Prize in Education, and her audience ran from Brandeis's Provost and some faculty members to a mob of students, mostly women.

I am a teacher, she began. Such a curtain raiser would sound saccha-rine in some settings. Somehow in this one it did not. The assertion came across as a strong declarative sentence, neither a whine nor the prelude to a virulent attack on "the system."

I am a teacher, and teaching, she asserted, is a glorious craft. Michele's speech had a smooth and persuasive cadence, which was no surprise as she certainly had given a version of it hundreds of times. Being the National Teacher starts with an award in the Rose Garden of the White House and is followed by a grueling year of visits all across the country, touting the profession. She had to have a stump speech, and this apparently was it.

Michele must have been wonderful at spreading her message. She had a presence, welcoming yet formal, confident but not overbearing. For her Brandeis audience she was also very personal, telling us about several of her students and why and how they had moved her. She described her classroom at a regional high school in Vermont, a place that clearly was her sanctuary, her place, hers alone. There were tables, not individual desks. She chose to cluster them, making classes into conversations not only between her and her pupils but also among the pupils themselves. There were plants, pictures, books, and peanut butter and crackers always available for kids who came to school hungry.

Michele taught social studies, up and down the high school curriculum. She spoke most fondly of her Advanced Placement United States History classes and of a particular excursion with kids to Washington that was both hilarious and moving, and, for some of us schoolfolk, familiar. To save money, for example, the buses traveled both to and fro at night, the assumption being that the kids might sleep then and not require motel rooms for two nights in Washington. Of course few did sleep, most preferring to gab, thereby arriving in the District of Columbia a ragged mob. And yet many were reverential at Washington's monuments; Michele recalled particularly the quiet discussions that she had with awed students at the Lincoln Memorial.

She described sending her students out to study the old barns and houses of an earlier Vermont, making drawings, calculating sizes, getting the stories of the oldsters still there. She reveled in the youngsters' realization that history was everywhere, even in the rural north. Textbooks were available, but only as reference books; Michele had the students read primary and secondary sources that she had selected, drawn from many quarters. Student mastery had to be more than just what was on "some standardized test," Michele argued. Such tests, especially of reading ability, told her something some of the time about a student, but the homogenized history tests did not go richly enough into the discipline to meet her standard. She measured each student's progress in varied ways, one by one.

Michele accomplished all this while being a spouse, mother, and continuing scholar. Some might call Michele a Super Woman, but I am sure that she would dismiss that characterization. She did, however, warmly acknowledge the support of her family for her work.

I am a teacher. And mightily proud of it. The young in that Brandeis audience might have concluded, however, that Michele had it all, and that "all" was likely to be a rare occurrence. They knew that half of all new teachers left the profession within five years. Clearly there was something unappealing out there. Michele bore witness to the Brandeis undergraduates that a vibrant professional life is very possible, however, even in a community not awash with wealth and political clout.

My older, more seasoned eye saw something more in the picture of Michele and her school. Michele clearly had *authority,* authority in the sense that she had substantial control over her work and workplace. This control was not so much of a bureaucratic kind, such as that found in collective bargaining agreements and in school districts where no one can wholly trust another—usually with good reason, given the faceless scale of most such systems. It was control born of respect by others—school authorities, colleagues, parents, and students—for Michele's particular, personal professionalism.

She had her own classroom that she could equip and adorn in ways that reflected her expectations. She could get the books she wanted for her particular students. Although she was influenced by state curricular frameworks, she was not their slave, and the "higher" authorities apparently did not object when she devoted substantial periods of time to local history, matters that were unlikely to find their way onto tests sent down from above. Michele had substantial control over her professional world. It clearly had been a tonic.

Such authority arises inevitably from powerful personal idiosyncrasy—constructive individualism—and idiosyncrasy is the enemy of bureaucratic systems that require predictable behavior. Michele handles her students in one way; another equally successful teacher may have a sharply differing style.

How messy! Or so it would appear to some. If Michele had her own room, thus left empty of students when she was not actually teaching, wasn't that a waste of space? Can the district afford "empty" classrooms? If Michele focused one year on (say) the American Civil War and Reconstruction, including a trip to Washington and perhaps to Gettysburg or Antietam, what was not thereby "covered" in her classes? If it was not "covered," might her kids thereby be at risk with the statewide American History tests that "covered" Pocahontas to Dick Cheney? If Michele received "special treatment," should not every person in her department receive measurably equal treatment, or "equal" after longevity within the district was taken into account?

How could one efficiently and fairly "score" the results of local history projects? If no one could "rank" the students and assign precise numbers to that ranking, how could these projects be used to assign "rank in class"? Those crackers and peanut butter could attract ants and mice as well as the enmity of other teachers who felt that it was not their job to feed children so disorganized that they failed to eat breakfast at home. If Michele got special deals, such as a year's leave to be Teacher of the Year or permission to attend a scholarly institute, what about other teachers? Was her authority merely the clout arising from seniority? *Was it fair? Was it efficient?*

All this being asked, and legitimately so, Michele did exhibit the professional power that arises from warrantable confidence. She clearly worked within a system, within a gathering of fellow educators, and toward widely accepted general goals. In accomplishing this she discovered a rewarding and obviously effective personal practice, and thereby a career. In this practicing, however at times idiosyncratic, she gained the support, affection, and protection of her peers, bosses, and students.

Such authority must be earned. On the basis of proven competence, and within frameworks that were acceptable to her, Michele was given her head. She was respected because she understood her obligations, approaches, and style; and she did her complex job very well, and in a way that reflected the best of her.

She had a history. It counted. That it counted gave fuel to her continued professionalism. Her special professionalism strengthened her school and district. Everyone benefited.

Authority Distributed

Today in a school where authoritative, high-stakes decisions about students are expected, the conditions of work and expectations for each child are crucial. If I am expected to be an authority on each of my students, I must have no more youngsters for whom I am responsible than I can know well, in a secondary school fewer than eighty. I must be their teacher for a period long enough to make the necessary connections with each. I must be part of a group of teachers who share these same students because I need colleagues who may see things in a student that I miss or who are able to make connections that I do not. My colleagues and I need protected time for this sharing of evidence and impressions.

None of these conditions is at all unreasonable. No one would want to be judged, especially for high-stakes purposes, on less. Some schools, including public secondary schools with tight budgets, approach them, largely by putting such conditions at the head of the priorities list for both time and money and by eliminating programs of lower priority.

Nonetheless, these essentials are far from the reality of most of today's frenetic and over-complicated high schools. Even when told of schools that have established them, many on their faculties quickly, even mordantly, say, "Oh, we couldn't do that here." As a result, being a legitimate "authority" on one's students is nigh unto impossible in many of today's schools, and the expectation of so being and the incentive to pull it off are profoundly weak.

Further, these teachers continue, how can we be "authorities" when no one trusts us much anyway? Even if they did trust us there is little time to know each child well, much less to consult with colleagues about her or him. Test scores and grade-derived rankings are what the system wants, or at least uses. Report cards for my 150 kids this term? Understanding of each of my almost one thousand kids for whom I am expected to serve as "guidance counselor"? The best I can do is to fill in boxes on a form.

In spite of this justifiable and heartfelt lament, few teachers will ever argue that knowing one's students well is a matter of trivial importance. Sadly, it is just that they see little evidence that there is political will to act upon that imperative. Most school systems will not invest in it.

Where there is energetic reform today, a large school, for example, will be broken down into smaller, independent units, places where most of the adults know most of the kids. The record of such simple, well-focused schools with children drawn from every quarter, such as Fenway High School and other Pilot schools in Boston and the dozens of small high schools in New York City and Chicago, make a powerful case for this policy.[10] The children can be known well if such knowing is put as a nonnegotiable design principle, if the school is small enough so that all the teachers know each other, that most teachers know most of the students and their families, and that the regimen is flexible enough to accommodate the ever-shifting needs of particular students.

Teachers can thereby be *authorities* on their students. They can "know" each of them in varied ways, not just as names or as children of a certain age or as students placed in a class on the basis of only a "grade" or a "score."

Authority Tested

I attended my first sit-in in New York City, at the Joan of Arc Junior High School in Manhattan. It was the mid-1960s. I wasn't sitting in. I was being sat in on, or, rather, my hosts at the school were being sat on.

At the end of a teaching day we were on the stage of the school's auditorium for a parent, teacher, and community meeting. I was the Dean of the Harvard Graduate School of Education at the time, and the school's Principal, Edythe Gaines, was a part-time graduate student there. I had come to visit the school, to witness what Edythe planned as a parent/teachers' meeting, and to say a few congenial words to those assembled.

The particular issues that generated the big, unexpected turnout, largely of non-parents, are in retrospect not important. As I recall it, the matters causing community upset had to do with pupil assignments, but in those years they could have been about all sorts of kindred subjects, most then still within the discretion of a school principal and her teachers. The tension within this overwhelmingly African American crowd was evident, and the anger spilled into harsh rhetoric from speaker after speaker. We were expected to sit and to hear all that needed to be said, the time of day be damned.

I was frightened, not only by my immediate entrapment but also by the violence of some of the language. As I recall it, I sat at the side of the stage, dressed up Dean-like, crossing one leg over the other and then back, trying to be calm, or at least inconspicuous. Happily for me, the speakers ignored me totally. I was but a youngish white guy from some university who surely had no power.

People of all ages spilled over the uncomfortable fixed seats and into the corridors. Several rows of older males, some holding and periodically using the bullhorns, circled the walls. I can see Edythe standing quite still at the podium, courteous, steady, patient. She let people talk. She did not interrupt. She waited, and waited some more. Her calm composure, so illuminated by her posture, personified respect, patience, and conciliatory style, in time drained enough of the anger so that the meeting could disperse.

That posture, and the wisdom it represents, sticks with me. It remains complex and ever admired. Her stillness signaled confidence. Her formality signaled respect. These qualities surely made it possible for her to keep control of the microphone on the stage, and thus the meeting, save for the bullhorns in the hands of some of the protesters. Her courage, patience, and wisdom were palpable. For all I know, she may have been shaking in her high heels. However, she exhibited no such panic. What she did exhibit was authority, in this mid-1960s situation, both to gather her immediate community and to act on her judgment as to what was best for all the constituencies within her school, not only those gathered before her at this moment. And in those days, she had substantial discretion to act as she saw fit.

The authority exercised by Edythe in that junior high school auditorium was deliberate. She *chose* to act in the way she did, and she had the power to act. The end she sought was a gathering of parental commitment to the work of the school. By calling such a meeting, knowing that it might be restless (she had no inkling of the "takeover," however), she expressed power, her power, her ability to shape events for the benefit of the children and families in her school's community.

Four decades later, Edythe's successors have far less authority. Power, and the detailed decisions about its exercise, has been moved up the educational hierarchy since the late 1960s, first to districts, then to the states, and, with the passage of the No Child Left Behind Act of 2001, to the Federal government. The implicit message is that those below have been found wanting, so wanting that effective repairs by those lower levels are neither expected nor contemplated. Today, the *expression of authority*—power—is to an unprecedented degree now found in the form of regulation and threat. High government will set the standards, insist on the shape of the programs, and test the students to ascertain whether the ends desired are being met. If high government is unsatisfied, public humiliation follows (scores published, schools labeled) and eventually heads roll.

It does not have to be this way. A carefully crafted system of balanced authority can protect both the obligations of central government and the conditions that allow the Edythes, Phils, and Micheles to display their idiosyncratic authority—and to attract and hold other strong people like them into the system. The people on the front lines need the structural framework that central government might provide, and central government needs the devotion and craftsmanship of topflight frontline people.

The evidence is there. So is common sense, and a flood of stories of what does not work effectively and what might. What is disappointing is the silence of the system's leaders in acting decisively on this evidence.

3 Order

In a class called "The American School," which I took from Associate Dean Judson Shaplin at Harvard in the fall of 1956, we were honored by a visit from the then-Superintendent of the Boston Public Schools, Frederick Gillis. With confident pride and good humor, he extolled the virtues of his district's work in a variety of ways, one of which has stuck with me.

Gillis admired order and predictability, and he proclaimed that it was a school system's obligation to arrange for it. He told us, for example, that on any morning of any week he knew exactly what every second grade student in every Boston elementary school was studying. The regimen was all laid out, neat and tidy. All the teachers had to do was to carry it out.

Although even at that time I found this a caricature, it was nonetheless wonderfully charming, totally memorable, even down to the man's friendly stance behind the laboratory table in Mallinkrodt Chemistry Building where large Education courses in those days were conducted. Here was this unthreatening, genial, genuinely concerned superintendent who had regulated his school system in such detail that he knew the every word and the every move assigned each of his pedagogical foot soldiers on any morning.

Caricature though this might have been, Gillis's descendants are alive and well. I met some of them at a late-1990s conference on school reform held not in chemical-smelling Mallinkrodt but in the elegant penthouse of the A. Alfred Taubman Building of Harvard's John Fitzgerald Kennedy School of Government. The sponsor was the School's Center for Business and Education, and the gathering was in honor of David Kearns, the retired CEO of Xerox and Under Secretary of Education during the first Bush administration. I was on a panel of educators and education industry executives.

All of us panelists agreed, not surprisingly, that America needed "rigorous schooling arising from high standards," in the accepted jargon of those times. The rub came with what that aphorism practically meant, whether there could and should be a single, national meaning and representation of "high standards" and who should decide these matters. The last of our speakers was the CEO of a fast-growing national education tutoring and Charter school operation business. She was clearly frustrated. "My company cannot make money if the product is not specified and national," she insisted. "Without a common curriculum, common assessments, and predictable scale we cannot succeed" (or words to that effect).

From her business perspective, there had to be *order*. Without order —standard expectations, standard products, and standard assessments, ones that would have warmed Gillis's heart— "reform" as she defined it, and as she wished to engage her company in it, could not happen. Education had to be universally predictable, what the historian David Tyack once described as a "One Best System."[1]

Americans have long been on a search for order, especially in communities composed of peoples from varied geographic, racial, and religious quarters. Public education has been perceived as a pivotal mechanism, often the prime mechanism, for such order, the "balance-wheel of the social machinery" of republican government, as Horace

Mann put it in 1848.[2] The worries expressed by our Kennedy School panel had substantial antecedents. As an historian, I long had a special interest in how Americans tried to use schools as an engine for order. As an educator, I fancied the notion of schools being "balance wheels." I understood the benevolence that undergirds this effort: we create this order for you, young person, so that you learn well and thus become free.

To all too many in our time, however, "order" in schools has in effect meant the *appearance* of order: a clearly demarcated district plan, a fully outlined step-by-step curriculum, complete with local, state, and Federal "benchmarks" for students and teachers to meet, quiet hallways, a low hum of teachers explaining things, an absence of graffiti and litter, well-groomed students, unruffled principals, a generous cup of hot coffee and a quiet, uninterrupted briefing for visitors. Most of us who have lived in schools know, however, that such an appearance is a means, and often not the best means, to the end of orderly minds.

There is plenty of noise these days about the necessity of order in schools and a frightening *silence* about what it takes to help shape orderly minds. The hard, familiar reality is that learning is both idiosyncratic (you and I do not learn everything in quite the same way and pace) and messy. Most serious learning is not nicely sequential; rather, it often spirals, with each of us circling back—if we have the opportunity—again to where we thought we were but, ideally, now better informed and thereby finding ourselves at a deeper place. It is situational, depending on immediate conditions for each of us as individuals and the appropriateness of our surroundings. The order that we seek to find in a school is a means to the end of order in each student's mind.

Over time, "order" for me has become both an essential concept in education and a pejorative. Two men profoundly influenced me in my struggle with this contradiction.

Ten Wise Men

The first was Charles William Eliot. I never actually met him, but I read his mail.

It would have been difficult for me to talk with him, as he died in 1926. The closest I came was through my father who, while an undergraduate at Harvard College before the First World War, remembered seeing the old gentleman—Harvard's President from 1869 to 1909—riding his bicycle in Cambridge. Eliot was easy to spot, as he had an authoritative carriage and a pronounced birthmark on his face.

I read Eliot's mail while doing the research for my doctoral thesis on the 1893 Report of the Committee of Ten on Secondary School Studies of the National Educational Association (now called National Education Association, simplified as NEA) of which Eliot was Chair.[3] Eliot's personal and institutional papers were largely in the Harvard University archives. A chemist by training, Eliot wrote in spare and sometimes breathtakingly direct prose. His attention to the rapidly growing number of academies and high schools arose naturally from his Harvard duties, as well-prepared freshmen would become interesting and adept students at his College. By the end of the 1880s his interest in secondary education clearly deepened. He accepted the opportunity to speak to various school groups and in 1890 published an influential essay prepared for the NEA on "The Gap between the Elementary Schools and the Colleges," an essay that brought him a national audience.

The Committee of Ten emerged from conversations among university leaders who in those times dominated the politics of the NEA. Behind all this talk was the young academic entrepreneur Nicholas Murray Butler of Columbia University; it was Butler who persuaded Eliot to take charge of the work, and it was at Columbia that the Committee met. The Ten included the philosopher, ex–school superintendent, and then United States Commissioner of Education William Torrey Harris, and a mix of men who were currently serving as college presidents, college professors, or high school teachers and administrators. Two of these college presidents had earlier been teachers and secondary school principals. James Baker of the University of Colorado, for example, had been Principal of the Yarmouth, Maine, High School and of Denver High School. Richard Henry Jesse of the University of Missouri had been a high school teacher of French and mathematics. The schoolmen came from well-established institutions, ones that "prepared" students for higher education. For example, John Tetlow was the Principal of Girls' Latin School in Boston. James Cameron Mackenzie was Headmaster of Lawrenceville School in New Jersey. Oscar Robinson taught Latin and Greek at Albany High School in New York. For its time the Committee was nationally representative, and it reflected its age in that all its members were Caucasian males. These were men with clout, none more so than Eliot. Ten Wise Men.

What concerned the NEA and its Committee was the apparent *disorder* in the transition from school to college. Even age grading itself was a relatively new practice in many small high schools, and more than a few colleges felt the need (academic and financial) to provide "preparatory" courses for their incoming students. Course titles had many meanings.

The Committee was gathered to recommend order. It shrewdly drew from existing practices in the most respected places. It provided for some variety, but not too much; a student would enroll in one of four sequences—Classical, Latin-Scientific, Modern Languages, or English. It built its curriculum around the "mainline" subjects (Eliot's term) of English, mathematics, foreign language, history, and science. Thanks to Harris, it arranged for the United States Office of Education to print ten thousand copies of the complete report and to send them free to as many American high schools as possible—a "first" in what, a hundred years later, is the routinely expected frenzy of "dissemination" of a national committee's findings.

For me the quintessence of the Report resided in the four tables that the Committee crafted to express its convictions in bold and practical terms.[4] What these tables assume without much discussion —indeed, with the tacit assumption that they were obvious matters— is important, for those assumptions (if not the Ten's particular prescriptions) have become deeply embedded in the way that Americans think about and thus craft their secondary schools. The practices following on the assumptions would bring order.

Again, the Committee did not invent these notions. They were abroad in the most respected secondary schools. What the Committee did was to make them totems, ones that we employ to this day virtually without thinking. Lamentably, several simply do not survive scrutiny, and the extent that they persist radically narrows the ways that we think about, and ultimately act on behalf of, schools.

Three of these assumptions are critical.

The first is the metaphor of school as the *deliverer* of skills and knowledge. We design schools as lists of offerings, like "English," and we list what books should be read, what material should be "covered," what topics should be tested in each area. In our time, scores of committees create these great lists of what is to be delivered, these lists now gussied up as "curriculum frameworks." Such lists are fun to design, fascinating to second guess ("Why didn't that committee in 1998 include more study of Islam?"), and useful in that they give some guidance to the "deliverers," that is, the teachers.

The problem is that what we teachers deliver is nice but in the long run secondary. Ultimately, what is relevant is only what the student knows, can do, and is in the habit of doing. For the adolescent to recite a list back to us is little more than evidence that he has memorized that list. However, we wish for more: the practical and resourceful *use* of that which might be on the list, especially in new situations, because the culture and the economy, inconveniently, do not stand still. Virtually nowhere, either in the Report of the Committee of Ten or in most later documents, save in hortatory rhetoric, is this complex end of the thoughtful exploitation of knowledge honored.

A traditional curriculum of coverage stops before it is useful. The philosopher Alfred North Whitehead said it well in 1929: "A merely well-informed man is the most useless bore on God's earth."[5] The well-informed person should have been able to *use* the information obtained, in sophisticated ways. The Committee of Ten's curriculum stopped with a list of what was to be *delivered* in school; the Committee did not ponder what might be needed for students to *use* that knowledge when confronted by new situations.

The Committee's approach set a pattern. The 1983 influential national report *A Nation At Risk* reflected it—and fell into the same trap as had Eliot. Its suggestions, eerily similar to those of the Ten, were cast in terms of what the schools should provide along with vague language about the intellectual qualities required by an internationally competitive workforce.

The metaphor of delivery can become a curse on educators' thinking. It is reasonable, indeed essential, as a point of departure, but, if it is used as the only metaphor, especially the central metaphor, for school, it cheapens the enterprise.

A second problem arises from the Committee's use of *time* as the coinage of school. Classes are described in terms of minutes expended, these packaged as "periods" by the Committee, each student engaged in twenty-five to thirty-three periods per week. The more important the subject, the more minutes it deserved. The students in the first year of the Classical program, for example, had Latin five periods a week and History four periods. A second-year student in the Modern Languages track would have four periods for German or French and three for geometry.

The tables in the report of the Committee of Ten describe in detail the time that each subject would be assigned, the metric being the "numbers of classes." A "class" existed when students and teacher were gathered for a prescribed "period" of time, usually an hour, for the former to be exposed to the subject by the latter. The Ten designed four programs, the Classical being the flagship and the English being the least demanding. In between were programs of middling demand titled Latin-Scientific and Modern Languages. All had offerings of each of the "mainline" subjects, with different emphases, these represented by time. The fourth year (twelfth grade) of the Classical program, for example, had Latin (four periods per week), Greek (five periods), English (two periods), German or French (three periods), Chemistry (three periods), and Trigonometry and Higher Algebra or History (three periods). The second year (tenth grade) of the English program will be more familiar to early twenty-first-century readers: English (three or five periods), Geometry (three periods), Physics (three periods), Latin, German, or French (four or five periods), History (three periods), and Botany or Zoology (three periods).[6]

By modern standards even the English program is a substantial academic feast. However, that is not my point here. What is here to note is the coinage of time. It is time—time in "periods," minutes in class—that counts. And the time accumulated in these periods leads to "years," a dedication of academic time in school for each of successive twelve-month periods. For the Committee of Ten, every student was to complete his or her chosen program in four years.

All this is very neat, as neat as the markings of the minutes on an old-fashioned pocket watch. The damnable problem is that no one of us learns, in whatever fashion, in precisely the same period of time. As an eighth grader, my heart froze when I heard Mrs. Hitchcock, our teacher, say to me and my classmates, "It's quiz time!" She turned to the board and wrote a question. "You have ten minutes." Pause. "Now, Go!" The hearts of some of my quick-working classmates leapt with joy. Another chance to show off how good we are! For me, the set time was paralyzing. Whatever good work I produced as an early teenager emerged from slow, time-consuming toil. Timed tests were a poor demonstration of what in fact I could do.

If the end is learning by each student, the time expended to get there has to some practical degree to reflect each particular learner at each moment. Some of us are "fast" learners, in some subjects but perhaps not others, and some are "slow." The time each one takes and when he or she takes it are major factors. On a Monday morning I may be sleepy and inattentive, but on a Wednesday I am brimming with energy. For the teacher and for the distant curriculum planner, that is terribly inconvenient. As did the Committee of Ten, schools today accommodate kids like me by creating "Honors" tracks for the apparently swift (or politically well connected) and "Regular" and "Special" tracks for the apparently less apt. Overall most schools judge their students on how well they "do" in a prescribed, consistent period of time. Indeed, in some situations "more time" is considered "unfair."

What to do? This is a solvable problem. Clarify what the student is expected to show (that is, know and use) in order to receive (say) a high school diploma. Insist, assist, and cajole every young person to work toward this target as attentively as possible. Assess the progress of each student regularly. Recognize the student's hitting of the target when in fact he hits it, and not before or far after his work entitles the hit, whatever his chronological age. None of this is arcane. I am describing what good soccer coaches and violin teachers do routinely with each of their players.

Is such practice totally impractical? No, but it is surely complex. It forces tough issues of content and quality, of not only what is to be "covered" but also how to know if a young person has made useful sense of it all. Students will have to be taken one by one, just like patients in a good hospital and candidates for drivers' licenses in sensible departments of motor vehicles. "Progress by performance" is found in a growing number of schools today and particularly in the home schooling movement. The process is necessarily cumbersome but far more sensible than the inefficient and profoundly discriminatory time-driven/age-delimited system that we have now.

I have had many opportunities over the past two decades to make the preceding argument. Few disagree with it. Few choose to follow its logic into decisive practice, however, and the worship of "time" continues in most schools today. With minutes as coins, the creation of "a school day" is a ready and standardizable possibility. It is superficially rational. It certainly appears orderly. It has the weight of tradition behind it: Eliot lives. However, it flies in the face of both common sense and generations of research on human learning.

A third residue in our thinking about schooling that arises in considerable part from the Report of the Committee of Ten has to do with what we have come to call *subjects*. What Yale College's President Jeremiah Day insisted in 1828 to be "the discipline and the furniture of the mind" has been codified over time into spheres of knowledge, these in turn evolving into topics, and thence into sequences of topics.[7]

We still struggle with this matter of subjects—perhaps better described as a *structure of knowledge* or *disciplines*—as much as did President Day, perhaps more so as our generation's expectations for a competent and principled citizen are broader and deeper than was the case while John Quincy Adams was president. By the 1890s, however, there was a consensus among academics about what were the main lines at least of the furniture of the mind. These lines developed widely accepted titles: English. Classical and Modern Foreign Languages. Mathematics. Science. History. Geography. Most were broken down into subspecialties: for example, Physics, Chemistry, Biology, Botany, Physiology, Arithmetic, Algebra, Geometry, Trigonometry, Higher Algebra. In due course each of these was reduced to lists of topics and texts. These were folded into sequences of classes to be delivered to the students.

Such codification makes sense. There is order in knowledge, and our pursuit of the shape of that order has been never ending. Like most deeply important things in our world, however, the codifying of knowledge is in constant movement, affected both by new research findings and by cultural tastes. If one takes scholarship seriously, there can never be, alas, One Best Stable Predictable Course of Study Forever.

The "main lines" identified by the Committee of Ten (and regularly given fresh oxygen by such groups as the 1983 *Nation At Risk* committee) are not necessarily the best, much less the only pattern that leads most efficiently toward the discipline and furniture of adolescent minds.

Just what, for example, is "English"? A list of "good" books to be mastered? An ability to write clearly and, with special effort, some grace? If this is so, might it be true that "History" is also a list of "good" books and an ability to express thoughts about them and their stories? Perhaps. There is analysis required in both English and History. Of course. Is there analysis required in Science? Of course. One must observe carefully, measure, weigh, and ponder systematically. But don't you do just that in English and History? Of course. So, why separate the subjects? The binomial theorem, *King Lear,* and the Battle of Hastings are very different phenomena. Does the way I think in each of the three profoundly differ from that of the others? Yes, but perhaps in ways that fall differently from what is reflected in the main line secondary school curriculum.

The definition of the curriculum is all the more complicated, as scholars in every field of serious knowledge have persuasively argued for most of the past three decades.[8] The interaction of individual minds and hearts and expressions of reality, whether the television pictures of New York on September 11, 2001, or reports of the unraveling of the human genome, provokes deep and often chaotic, even irrational, reactions. Presumably schooling is in large part about valuing the rational and its ways. How those ways are developed in each young citizen is far more complex than represented in the routines of most schools. A particular mischief is embedded in the metaphor of "coverage," and most school, district, and state curricula compound that error by asking that more be "covered" than can be to meet a worthy standard for all but the most dutiful and favored students.

Nonetheless, *on paper* the standard curriculum gives the impression of order, even if the reality is far more complex. The blunt assurance on these matters provided by the Committee of Ten and its membership of influential establishment authorities gave it political and professional authority. Then and now, however, the codification of "subjects" followed by lists of matter to cover, books to read, and skills to develop obscures the complexity of the task of teaching. It makes the educator's work appear far simpler than it actually is, and it leads to a course of study that, for most students, is shallow. In an ironic and curious way, the authorities must surely know that it is shallow—the evidence is all around us—which makes the costs even more poignant.

None of this lessens the contribution of the Committee of Ten. Charles William Eliot's relentless work reflected both arrogance and imagination. The arrogance was reflected in the certainty with which he asserted all sorts of educational "truths," most of these far beyond the scope of his personal discipline as a chemist. The imagination was reflected by his recognition that little in the way of reform would emerge from merely an essay on the state of secondary education, however brilliant. What was needed were specific marching orders. The Ten provided them in the four tables, especially Table 4, which set forth four related programs from which high schools could choose.

Later reports, particularly the NEA's 1918 Committee on the Reorganization of Secondary Education, appeared to have jettisoned key parts of the Ten's proposal, largely by the introduction of more "practical" subjects.[9] This is undoubtedly true in some respects, but what Eliot's successors did not challenge were the key ways in which Americans should comprehend schooling. The metaphor of delivery, the coinage of time, and the reduction of learning to discrete "subjects" persisted—even if the subject was Cosmetology.

Eliot had kept it simple, had kept it practical, had made it specific right down to the numbers of "periods" a "subject" would be taught on a school day. Copy one of these four programs, he implied, and you will not go wrong. Overworked school boards, superintendents, and principals all across the country, overwhelmed by a sudden interest in schooling beyond the rudiments and buttressed by an economy that both yielded new tax revenues and lessened the need for adolescents' labor, gratefully cleaved at least to the structure of the blueprint, decade upon decade.

One Wise Man

Charles William Eliot's arrogance and imagination have always intrigued me. During the 1970s and early 1980s I met those qualities again, this time in flesh and blood, in the person of Mortimer J. Adler.

Adler, a crusty and controversial public intellectual, delivered to me an invitation via a Phillips Academy student of mine, John Van Doren. Would I join the Paideia Group?

I had heard of Adler and had read a bit of what he had written, but I had only the vaguest sense of the man and his passions, much less the Paideia Group. I knew that he was living in Chicago and was associated with the *Encyclopaedia Britannica,* as were several adult Van Dorens. John was in a senior History seminar that I was teaching; John's father had joined Adler in a "group" to discuss, debate, and recommend a future shape of American public education. Adler carefully chose the word *Paideia:* it came, he told us, "from the Greek *pais, paidos:* the upbringing of the child . . . In an extended sense, the equivalent of the Latin *humanitas* . . . signifying the general learning that should be the possession of all human beings."[10] I signed up.

Most of the Group's meetings, each of a couple of days, were held at the Wye Plantation of the Aspen Institute in Maryland. Adler had assembled a group of academic luminaries but perhaps felt that it was a bit short on people who had some sense of the realities of the schools. Among others, I was to be one of those people.

Adler was in the chair, figuratively and physically. His principal sparring partners were Jacques Barzun, Clifton Fadiman, James O'Toole of the University of Southern California, and three Van Dorens— John, Charles, and Geraldine—Dennis Gray of the Council for Basic Education, Theodore Puck of the Eleanor Roosevelt Institute for Cancer Research, and Otto Bird of the University of Notre Dame. School people were members of the Group, but their attendance was spotty due to their high-pressure jobs: Superintendents Alonzo Crim of Atlanta and Ruth Love of Chicago, and Nicholas Caputi, the Principal of Skyline High School in Oakland, California. Two college presidents were included, Leon Botstein of Bard and Adele Simmons of Hampshire. In all, we numbered twenty-two.

The talk circled again and again over familiar ground. Adler kept pushing us back to the ideas of the three men to whom the report was ultimately to be dedicated: Horace Mann, John Dewey, and Robert Hutchins. We talked and argued, often over minutiae, with the most explosive disagreements being between the idealist Adler, who believed with the fervor of Mann in universal public education, and the elitist Barzun who (though he never put it as bluntly) felt that both Adler and Mann were naive. Only slowly did I realize that the Group was not to write a report. Adler was. Our function was to provoke Adler, thereby deepening his ideas.

The result was a volume, published in 1982, of fewer than eighty pages. It was prefaced by simple assertions. "We are politically a classless society." Adler wrote. "Our citizenry as a whole is our ruling class. We should, therefore, be an educationally classless society."

He went on: "We should have a one-track system of schooling, not a system of two or more tracks, only one of which goes straight ahead while others shunt the young off onto sidetracks not headed toward the goals our society opens to all. The innermost meaning of social equality is *substantially the same quality of life for all*. That calls for: *the same quality of schooling for all*." (The italics are Adler's.)

"We must end the hypocrisy in our national life. We cannot say out of one side of our mouth that we are for democracy and all its free institutions including, preeminently, political and civil liberty for all; and out of the other side of our mouth, say that only some of the children—fewer than half—are educable for full citizenship and a full human life. . . . There are no unteachable children. There are only schools and teachers and parents who fail them."[11]

The Paideia Proposal was appropriately subtitled *An Educational Manifesto*. Adler wanted it to be an abrupt and compelling declaration, one that would catch the imagination of Americans by going back to democracy's first principles. Like Eliot before him, he wanted it to be simple enough to be practical and sophisticated enough to reflect reality. There was far more flourish to Adler's prose than that which had emerged from the Committee of Ten. The rhetoric was worthy of an oration. Again like Eliot, Adler bristled with confidence.

Once again a chart emerged, this one divided into three columns reflecting neither students' ages nor subjects of the curriculum (as had the 1893 Report). Rather, they represented "three distinct modes of teaching and learning, rising in successive graduations of complexity and difficulty from the first to the twelfth year." All three were deemed "essential" for every child. There was to be the same course of study for all, "course of study" being implied by the contents of the three columns.

Column One denoted the "acquisition of organized knowledge . . . by means of Didactic Instruction," including lectures, textbooks, and "other aids" in three grand areas, "Language, Literature, and the Fine Arts . . . Mathematics and Natural Science . . . [and] History, Geography, and the Social Studies." So far, he more or less trod the paths of the Committee of Ten.

Column Two was identified as the "Development of Intellectual Skills—Skills of Learning . . . by means of Coaching, Exercises, and Supervised Practice . . . in the operations of . . . Reading, Writing, Speaking, Listening . . . Calculating, Problem-Solving . . . Observing, Measuring, Estimating . . . Exercising Critical Judgment." Here Adler was on ground little covered by Eliot.

Column Three—Adler's special joy—dealt with the "enlarged understanding of ideas and values . . . by means of . . . maieutic or Socratic questioning and active participation . . . in the . . . discussion of books (not textbooks) and other works of art and involvement in artistic activities e.g., Music, Drama, Visual Arts." Adler would include a specific jab at textbooks—he favored original texts—and would add a word like "maieutic," one that sent me tumbling to the dictionary. (It means, according to the *American Heritage Dictionary,* "Of or relating to the aspect of the Socratic method that induces a respondent to formulate latent concepts through a dialectic or logical sequence of questions.")[12] Adler reveled in the intellectual ping-pong over ideas arising from specific texts. He must have despaired of the often rootless debates in which his group engaged.

Two more Paideia books followed. *Paideia Problems and Possibilities: A Consideration of Questions Raised by the Paideia Proposal,* published in 1983, was his restless answer to his critics. *The Paideia Program: An Educational Syllabus,* which appeared in 1984, was a collection of "how-to" essays, including a piece on coaching that I had written. Some of us pursued the Paideia ideas actively, none more than Dennis Gray, who trained hundreds of school teams in how to run a Socratic seminar. Although Adler was never successful in getting a whole university school of education to take the group's ideas seriously, a few picked up the matter and are still hard at work in Paideia centers today.[13] I used the Paideia work in 1984 as an organizing arrangement of ideas in *Horace's Compromise.*

Sadly, while the Paideia Group's ideas flickered for some months, they never had the staying power anticipated for them by Albert Shanker, the president of the American Federation of Teachers, who predicted that the *Proposal* "would dominate education discussion for the next decade."[14] Adler's flinty personality had something to do with it. He had little patience with what he believed to be sloppy-thinking folks. Even though the text was deliberately short and blunt, it never attracted the interest of book lovers' discussion groups or education activists. The Group was composed neither of nationally known public educators nor a person with political leverage such as Eliot had in William Torrey Harris, the U.S. Commissioner of Education. The ideas did not fit neatly into any Education school program.

Nonetheless, Adler's chart, and the ideas it adumbrated, remains important. It was a provocation, not a road map. It insisted that school people *think;* it did not tell them exactly what to do in their schools with that thought. It was not something to "put into place," in the easy jargon of our time. It did not frontally address schools' problems as educators defined those problems. Actually, it added to those educators' burdens by asking them to ponder anew and deeply about the direction of their public enterprise. It was, thereby, dismissed as impractical.

All that being said, Adler was closer to the heart of the matter of serious schooling in a democracy than had Eliot been. Although it did not specify any contrary view, the *Proposal* did not accept and use education's bad habits and faulty metaphors as had the Committee of Ten. Rather, Adler implied that thoughtful educators would inevitably recognize the costs of the metaphor of "delivery" as the only manner of teaching, of the rigidity of an institution constructed primarily by the allocation of time, and of the distortion of scholarship arising from a secondary school curriculum broken into impermeable academic subjects.

Adler deserved better. The education establishment, barely reading —much less pondering—his work, let him down. He was dismissed as a prickly, out-of-touch, and narrowly "classical" (in the pejorative) philosopher. Or, more charitably, perhaps the establishment was fully, but quietly, aware of the implications of his manifesto. Much would have to change, especially the very way that educators defined teaching and learning. Such would require a revolution, not only in practice but also in the way a democracy views its duties toward its young. Such a move would, thereby, create disorder.

Order in Theory

The word "order" serves as both verb and noun.

As a verb it means to issue a command and as such is an active word. It shapes. It compels. It presses into arrangement. "I order you to wash the car."

As a noun, "order" is composed. It describes. It offers, again more or less, a shape. It just sits there, however, sometimes implying as much as limning what it specifically represents, like the balance reflected in a Hokusai print. The viewer makes what active sense of it that he wants. But before he acts, he has to think about it; he has to describe for himself precisely what to do.

The Committee of Ten was active. Its order was a verb. Here, the members said, is in detail what you should do. Get on with it.

The Paideia Group was passive. Its order was a noun. *The Paideia Proposal* described a human condition, a way to categorize and thereby to understand what it means to learn and to teach. The Group's proposals were a set of ideas, a suggestive arrangement rather than a strategy and a cluster of specified tactics. *The Paideia Program* that followed presented some images of what the ideas meant, but these carried no expectation of structural adoption. They were meant only as provocative examples.

Charles Eliot's time required a verb. Influential people believed both that Americans wanted many more high schools and that the existing institutions were ill designed. Accordingly, the Committee provided a plan. That plan caught hold, with a vengeance that the members could not have foreseen. Not all of what the Ten recommended survived, or was even faithfully represented, but the shape of the age-graded, time-driven, subject-described program, driven by a metaphor of delivery, took hold with extraordinary speed.[15] The times called for a verb. The Committee of Ten perceptively responded.

Adler's tactic was more oblique. *The Paideia Proposal,* he recommended, is a disciplined way to think about learning and teaching. Read it carefully. Create a seminar and debate, with all the constructive ferocity that would warm Socrates' heart. Only then—when you fully understand it both in its complexity and in your own appropriate terms—go forth and do something with it.

Unfortunately, Adler's time was indifferent to a proposal that presented itself as a noun. Late twentieth-century educational leaders appeared to think neither very hard nor very long about the substance of their work. Influential folks believed that they already knew what was needed and that Americans had to get on with that. They wanted a Plan, a System, something to "put into place."

Contemporary critics of education are apt to use adjectives like "soft" and "hard," "mindless" and "rigorous." Interestingly, both the 1893 *Report* and the 1982 *Proposal* have usually been categorized in the latter group—reports that are demanding and "academic." Such assignment is proper as both reports put serious and informed intelligence at the center of American democracy and of a thriving economy. The difference between the reports resides in the implication of each for "order." One is a detailed command for action; the other is an outline for rigorous reflection that would lead to actions arising from an affected community. As an American, the former distresses me; "order" in this sense of *imposition* is a pejorative. Order in the sense implied by Adler is both wise and essential.

I believe, then, for our times the Adlerian approach to "order" is to be favored. It is demanding; but it stresses the importance of free minds, of individual responsibility and creativity, and of the power of true democracy to create goodness—including "good" schools—from a process of invention rather than a predigested, imposed plan for education. Although Adler himself was among the most assured, and thus arrogant, of men, his plan reflects a trust in the People, in their necessary obligation to decide their own fates, which is poignant and profoundly democratic. Such faith is in short supply today, to democracy's peril.

Most participants at that late 1990s Kennedy School conference showed little interest in such matters. The statement by the CEO who needed standardized routines to shape her business was balefully crass. The processes of serious learning would be trivialized, reduced to uniform and predictable routines that could produce evidentiary test scores. Those routines were the basis of order; visible, predictable, standardized order was necessary, and the existence of that order presented a workable "market."

Further, most of the Kennedy School participants assumed without much thought that school was the primary, even the only, place where children could learn and that school would have a universal shape. Education began and ended with schooling, something that happened in a familiar, predictable, resource-requiring, and revenue-generating place. The conference unwittingly represented the poverty of turn-of-the-twenty-first-century thinking by American leaders on what a powerful education, an education worthy of a free people, can and should be.

Order by Mediation

Many Americans think hard about football. Most principals of most large high schools have to attend carefully—some very, very carefully —to their football teams, whether they want to or not. Most tax- and tuition-paying publics want victories.

Within days of the opening of school in my first year as a principal I deliberately wandered to the fields where Andover's team was practicing. Standing alone watching his boys work out was the school's storied coach Steve Sorota. I joined him. He took no notice. I took a stab at communication, trying to sound like an aficionado of Steve's complicated craftsmanship. "Have you a likely quarterback here?" No Sorota response, not even a slight bit of body language suggesting that he knew I was there. I waited, and then slunk away. "Nice to see you, Coach." No response.

Sorota turned out to be a warm friend. My mistake was even to suggest with a dumb question that I might invade his turf. He made sure that I knew exactly where that turf started and where it stopped. I learned to respect that.

Like most team sports and in spite of its messy expression, football is a carefully ordered game. Perhaps there are lessons here about "order" that transcend that sport.

Football has very specific rules and referees to enforce them. These rules set clear boundaries. However, within these boundaries each team is allowed—nay, expected—to devise its own best strategy and tactics. Although there are patterns, those tactics differ by team, even by year and by week.

Sorota had to build a program with the kids he was given. Tactics would differ if the quarterback was experienced and able to throw long and accurately or if he was green and equipped with an unsteady arm. Day to day, matters changed. A boy was ill or injured. A boy was failing a course and had to take a makeup test. Some boys did stupid things and were benched by a dean. Sorota had to improvise, often play by play. He had absolute authority to do so. For play on the field, no approval by the principal or any other interested party was necessary nor tolerated by a man with the experience and pride of Steve Sorota.

Nonetheless, for Steve there still were those general rules. When an official made what appeared to be a close call about a breach of a rule, Sorota or his deputies could contest that decision and ask for review. Professional teams have reduced this right to excruciating precision, with reruns of televised tape and time allotted for its painstaking review.

At that same time, the fans expected that the coach and his team would do what they had to do—in whatever way seemed best within the rules—to reach the highest level of play. Variety within the rules was a highly rewarded virtue. Engaged people will endlessly argue that football's rules are too numerous or not numerous enough, reasonable or unreasonable. Overall, however, football enthusiasts applaud a system of minimal, sensible rules and admire resourceful, original teams and their coaches.

If in football, why not in education? Why not a framework of rules, a set of referees (who fully expect that their judgments could be challenged), and an expectation that each school, given its particular situation—its size, its students, its faculty, its funding, and the mores of its community—would be designed and would function in its own best way? Principals would be like Steve Sorota: proud and experienced people who had and fully expected to keep their independence— albeit within overarching, demonstrably sensible but minimal rules.

The ways and means of providing social services and the organization of competitive football have a great deal not in common. Yet both face similar issues: the need for an orderly, fair common ground and the correlative need for local authority and wise diversity. Football, in its tiny little world, appears to have settled on a tolerated balance. Public services like schooling are nowhere close to a comparable balance and, indeed, exhibit little talk and less action about it.

In the late 1970s while I was at Andover and continually concerned about what should be the public role of a private school, I came upon an approach in the form of the argument by Peter L. Berger and Richard John Neuhaus in their short book *To Empower People: The Role of Mediating Structures in Public Policy.* The metaphor of *mediation* struck me—and still strikes me—as one constructive way to fill the silence in public policy for public education.

The Berger/Neuhaus argument, published in 1977, was simply outlined: "We suggest that the modern welfare state is here to stay, indeed that it ought to expand the benefits it provides—but that *alternative mechanisms are possible to provide welfare-state services.*"[16] They went on to recognize the existence of an "anti-government, anti-bigness mood [in the society] . . . impersonality, unresponsiveness, and excessive interference, as well as the perception of rising costs and deteriorating service." Their basic concept was the creation of "mediating structures" defined as *"institutions standing between the individual in his private life and the large institutions of public life."*[17] Mediating referees, perhaps? I wondered.

Their argument rested on three propositions. First: "Mediating structures are essential for a vital democratic society." To my educator's eye this is crucial: there must be a constructive balance between family specialness and collective democratic and economic needs.

Second: "Public policy should protect and foster mediating structures." That is, the state should not be passive about mediating structures that give life to private values. Rather, the state should actively assist their creation and vigorously protect them.

Third: "Whenever possible, public policy should utilize mediating structures for the realization of social purposes." That is, autonomous "street-level" private institutions (meaning places in charge of their own practice) can and should shoulder public obligations.[18]

Later in their essays, Berger and Neuhaus write bluntly of the schooling situation. "Most modern societies have in large part disenfranchised the family in the key area of education. The family becomes, at best, an auxiliary agency of the state, which at age five or six coercively takes over a child's education." They address the private school issue: "Of course there are private schools, but here class becomes a powerful factor. Disenfranchisement falls most heavily on lower-income parents who have little say in what happens to their children in school. This discrimination violates a fundamental human right, perhaps the most fundamental human right—the right to make a world for one's children. . . . Our purpose is not to deprive upper-income families of the choices they have. . . . Our purpose is to give those choices to those who do not now have decision-making power."[19]

As I read these last words, I recalled Edward Banfield's argument that there are some families—his "lower class"—that live in such disorganization that concern for the educational future of their offspring is far from their minds. Given options, many of those families would not know how or whether to take advantage of them. Although I feel that Berger and Neuhaus are, therefore, somewhat naive on this point, I still believe that the philosophical heart of their argument is correct. Disorganized and desperate families are a reality, but their existence neither trumps policies that are right for healthier families nor bespeaks any conclusion that state and private effort, imagination, and caring could not help such beleaguered families find some decent stability.

Berger and Neuhaus turn to policies that provide practical school choices for all families. They point out that "monopolies endowed with coercive powers do not change easily. The best way to induce change is to start breaking up the monopoly—to empower people *to shop elsewhere*. We trust the ability of low-income parents to make educational decisions more wisely than do the professionals who now control their children's education."[20]

There are ways beyond direct management wherein the state effectively remains a monopoly. A state, for example, could decide not to operate schools at all but still control the remaining so-called independent institutions with a blizzard of regulations, mandatory curriculum frameworks, and universal standardized examinations. The state thereby asserts that it knows, in substantial detail, what is best for the child but lets private entities carry out these centralized, standardized orders.

I doubt that such an omniscient state is what Berger and Neuhaus had in mind. The state—the People collectively—should retain some outer limits, such as decent, safe physical arrangements and programs that assure at least literacy, numeracy, and civic understanding, but, in the name of fundamental American freedom, it should allow "private" (family) interests substantial room to shape their own school communities. This requires restraint and good will on both sides, and it is this good will, this *trust*, as Deborah Meier has repeatedly reminded Americans, that is the primary fuel allowing mediating institutions to form and flourish.[21]

Berger and Neuhaus close their essays with an appeal for pluralism. "'E Pluribus Unum' is not a zero-sum game. That is, the *unum* is not to be achieved at the expense of the *plures*. To put it positively, the national purpose indicated by the *unum* is precisely to sustain the *plures*. Of course there are tensions, and accommodations are necessary . . . such tensions are not to be eliminated but are to be welcomed as the catalysts of more imaginative accommodations."[22]

One might conclude that Berger and Neuhaus were merely giving a fancy name to "choice" among schools, at least for those who can afford it. I believe that there is more to the idea. "Choice" can imply passivity. If you happen to want another school for your children than the one down the street, it is there, but you have to have the wit and energy and often the money to find it, and to get your youngster enrolled.

"Mediation" is a more active word. It connotes a process, a systematic—an *orderly*—means of relating and balancing the legitimate privacy of the family and the equally legitimate expectations of the People in general, represented by the state. A mediating institution would be Janus-faced, looking at once to the *unum* and the *plurum*, and balancing their claims.

The Berger/Neuhaus idea triggered others. For example, at the initiative of the American Enterprise Institute, which had sponsored the Berger/Neuhaus essays, David S. Seeley followed up with *Education Through Partnership: Mediating Structures and Education*, a careful and provocative analysis of what "mediation" might be within public education.[23] John E. Coons and Stephen D. Sugarman examined the legal and constitutional issues of "choice" in education in *Education by Choice: The Case for Family Control*.[24] Nonetheless, the disinterest in and often scathing hostility to these ideas by leaders in public education during the 1970s and 1980s kept their ideas at the margins of the advanced training of school leaders and off the agendas of professional meetings and school boards.

Signs of a change in popular attitudes, however, were apparent in the 1990s following on "best seller" status for David Osborne and Ted Gaebler's *Reinventing Government: How the Entrepreneurial Spirit Is Transforming the Public Sector*.[25] Osborne and Gaebler repeatedly use education as an example of a public enterprise stuck in frustrating mediocrity. In this new context, the late 1960s ideas of competition and "choice" for families reemerged, though now often cloaked in the mantra of a new conception of management and reflecting the furious assault on the existing system first provoked by the 1983 *Nation At Risk* report. The Berger/Neuhaus idea of new structures to forward families' "empowerment" was still alive.

Order as the Movement of Money

Money—who has it and how does it move—explains most of governmental policy. To put it baldly, richer Americans have most of the money and most of the say in how it moves. That is how a capitalist democracy works. The extent to which the People generally wish, for whatever reasons—charity or self-interest (stable communities, educated workforce, social tranquility)—to share the country's wealth is the extent to which the poor receive a worthy education, among other things, at public expense. How the money is to be spent in the service of the poor is a perpetual wrangle, the nature of which—even the language of which—provides a dependable barometer of Americans' priorities.

In 1965 I was asked by the Johnson administration to join a White House Task Force On The Cities to advise the President on policies to address what appeared to be growing chaos in our urban areas. The Congress had such a group under way, chaired by Senator Paul Douglas of Illinois. The Douglas effort was high profile and likely to nettle Johnson. The White House wanted a low-profile group quietly to plow the same ground and provide the President's staff with ideas and evidence independent of the Congress's work. I was as surprised as I was flattered to be asked to serve. Save for some research and writing that I was doing for a project led by Professor James Q. Wilson at Harvard on what he called "the metropolitan enigma," I was a neophyte on these matters.

Paul Ylvisaker was the Task Force's chairman. Paul traveled over two jobs during the Task Force's tenure, serving first as New Jersey's

Commissioner for Community Affairs and later as a staff member at the Ford Foundation. Other members of our group of eleven included Ivan Allen, the mayor of Atlanta, Edwin Berry of the Chicago Urban League; John Dunlop from Harvard's Department of Economics; and Ezra Ehrenkrantz of the Building Systems Development Corporation of California. Our focus was on four discrete topics: neighborhood centers, home ownership by the poor, the prospect of an Urban Development Corporation, and landlord-tenant relations. Schooling played a peripheral role. The Task Force was expected to get quickly into the sorts of details that could shape legislation. For most of the meetings, I necessarily acted the dutiful slightly-over-his-head student in a seminar taught by a clutch of highly experienced professors.

A theme that increasingly informed all our discussions (usually held very discreetly in the Old Executive Office Building) was that we should give "the poor" substantially more control over their lives. More services for their benefit from government was part of it, but equally important was how those services might be deployed—how the money was to move—in ways that were respectful of the recipients. For example, we recommended that the Neighborhood Centers' programs "be shaped from the standpoint of the individual's needs and not from a particular supplying agency's standpoint."[26] We made frequent references to various "voucher" schemes for housing and other services, especially those being discussed by the economist Milton Friedman. We talked often of how to get a modicum of significant initiative into the hands of poor families.

All this reminded me at the time that I was the beneficiary of the country's largest and most ambitious educational voucher scheme, the so-called G.I. Bill of Rights. Those of us who had served x months in the active military could apply for y months of tuition support for our education in federally approved schools, colleges, and universities. My twenty-two months of active duty translated—as long as I worked at full tilt—into the tuition for my entire graduate program at Harvard. With a growing family, Nancy and I knew just how crucial this was.

Without this federal program, my career in education would have been very different.

The G.I. Bill let me choose my graduate program, as long as it was on an approved list. The government sent the money (in response to Harvard's "vouchers" on my behalf) to the Comptroller of the university. My responsibility was to sign in with the Comptroller each month, to pass all my courses, and to keep my nose clean. Here was, in fact, an example of "mediation." The state provided the resources as long as I chose a governmentally approved institution; the institution provided the program of its own design; I provided the authorities at that approved institution with evidence of my progress. Here was a public end (an educated workforce) and a private means (I chose a university that had designed a program that gained approval from the state).

If this governmental device worked for me, was there an analogous program that might serve poor children? I worked up an idea for the Task Force that I deliberately called the Poor Children's Bill of Rights. Although it played no part in our recommendations to the President, our charge falling in somewhat different channels, I kept working on it and, ultimately and with the help of a Harvard graduate student, Phillip Whitten, published its outline in *Psychology Today* in August 1968.

Whitten and I summarized the idea: "Ours is a simple proposal: to use education—vastly improved and powerful education—as the principal vehicle for upward mobility. While a complex of strategies must be designed to accomplish this, we wish here to stress one: a program to give money *directly* to poor children (through their parents) to assist in paying for their education. By doing so we might create significant competition among schools serving the poor (and thus improve the schools) and meet in an equitable way the extra costs of educating the poor."[27]

Put differently, if the vouchers were *added* to existing per-pupil revenues, if these vouchers were large enough, and if intradistrict movement were allowed (as with Boston's METCO program, for example), a financial incentive would exist for all sorts of schools in the cities and in the suburbs to take poor kids. The fancy suburban high school could both salve its soul and add to its discretionary funds by admitting children from low-income families (should those families choose to apply). We larded the article with apt references across the political spectrum, from Paul Goodman to Milton Friedman. Our argument reflected the late 1960s priority of "racial and social class mixing" and a belief that a solid education is the necessary platform for a move out of poverty.

Upon publication, the article attracted some notice but quickly disappeared in the avalanche of news following on the murders of Martin Luther King Jr. and Robert Kennedy and on the expanding and increasingly unpopular Vietnam War. Rereading this article in 2003, it seems naive in its simplicity and optimism. Nonetheless, the idea persists. The Poor Children's Bill of Rights was specifically mentioned by Lamar Alexander in his run for the presidency in 2000 and continues to pop up occasionally. While the old details are now inapt, the notion of money following the child is still on the table. The argument has been distorted, however, by proposals that set the cash levels so low that they provide no incentive whatever save for certain nonpublic schools and thereby becoming an effective means of funneling moneys primarily into the private, religious, and for-profit sectors. For many advocates of truly public education, "voucher" has become, not surprisingly, a vile word, and the idea behind it a tactic for capturing public education for the private/religious and for-profit sectors.

It deserves better. Giving money to families is respectful; having bureaucracies tell them what to do in great detail is disrespectful. Competition among schools for dollars puts a premium on a faculty's imagination and performance; a lack of competition allows what is comfortable but inefficient to persist. The device *mediates*, giving families (private lives) and the schools (public institutions) each a part of the action. The practice mirrors the freedoms absolutely expected and carefully used by wealthier families, choosing where to live (often on the basis of the reputation of the local public schools) and whether to patronize a private school. If this works well for wealthier folks, why not for everybody?

There is a place for the money-following-the-child strategy in liberal as well as conservative politics. Indeed, for me that is the idea's particular strength. The tricky issue is how to arrange for it in an equitable and practical manner. To attach choice onto the existing systems is likely to be difficult. Perhaps the entire way that public schools are governed and financed, for rich and poor alike, needs clear-eyed examination.

Reordering the System

In 1997 I was asked by Frank Newman, then the President of the Education Commission of the States, to serve with sixteen others on the National Commission on Governing America's Schools. ECS is a not-for-profit creature of state governments, a think tank and convening authority serving the states with issues that transcend state borders. A rethinking of public school "governance" was such a timely task. The Commission's conclusions were to help policy makers and aid "the general public to make informed decisions about how to improve governance."

The Commission was co-chaired by Governor Paul Patton of Kentucky and James Renier, the recently retired CEO of Honeywell Corporation. Members were drawn from many quarters—teachers' unions (Adam Urbanski of Rochester, New York, and the American Federation of Teachers), academia (Lisbeth Schorr of the Harvard School of Public Health), state legislatures (Luther Olsen of Wisconsin), state and city Boards of Education (Thomas Davis of Missouri and Donald McAdams of Houston, Texas), and city school districts (Anthony Alvarado of San Diego, California). It had a slightly right-of-center tilt (reflecting the political temperature at the time), and it included David

Osborne, one of the authors of *Reinventing Government*. A key consultant was Paul Hill of the University of Washington and the RAND Corporation, who had written widely on matters of educational governance and control.

The Commission met in several venues and depended heavily on its members working over a series of drafts. Its report of some thirty pages, plus charts and graphs, was issued at Williamsburg, Virginia, in November 1999. All the Commission members—demonstrably a varied group—had signed it.[28]

The Commission proposed two "governance models"; however, both models had much in common. Each called for "strengthening, not discarding the public system of education." The fact that we had to start with that premise says worlds about the education policy climate in the late 1990s.

Next, however, came "allowing the money to follow the child to the school where he or she attends." This suggested budgetary authority moving downward, and the Commission expanded this by "granting individual schools control over their personnel and budget." What followed was "giving parents more choice about where their children attend school" and "providing good information on student, teacher and school performance for parents and the community." All schools were to be "of choice" and largely self-governing. "Redefining labor/management relations" and "focusing accountability systems on improved student achievement" followed. Precariously dangling at the end was a wan wish for "strengthening local school boards."[29]

What struck me then and now was not that any of these ideas was new but that this quite diverse late twentieth-century Commission had unanimously agreed to it. Furthermore, ECS is a very mainstream organization. "Choice," and thereby competition among schools, and decentralized budget control now appeared to be thoroughly centrist ideas.

In some quarters, the report was considered dangerous. The National School Boards Association, for example, arranged for substantial numbers of well-briefed members to attend our Williamsburg presentation and to voice strenuous, coordinated opposition. They accurately recognized that the Commission was threatening their existing powers and dignities.

Like most such efforts, the report was submitted, caused some ripples of interest, and then largely disappeared. ECS has kept at the work, however, providing some technical support to states wanting to try out these ideas. From my vantage point, the Report was a telling piece of evidence of how fragile the confidence in the status quo is even among a group of key "insiders."

Shortly thereafter, I had an opportunity to see how such ideas played out with a younger generation. Three of us serving as "visiting" teachers at Brandeis University in Waltham, Massachusetts, offered an education policy course, largely to undergraduates, in public school governance. My two colleagues were Jay Kaufman, an historian by training and a long-term member of the Massachusetts House of Representatives, and Sarah Cannon Holden, an attorney, mediator, and longtime leader in local government.

Jay arranged for a succession of state officials and experts to join our three-hour-long evening seminars. We drowned the students in books, including the ECS report, and asked them, in teams, to come up with a plan for the "governance" of a hypothetical county school district about which we gave them extensive data. (The county was, in fact, Massachusetts' Middlesex County, with the data simplified and rounded off.) Time and again the student teams saw the nub of the problem to be a balance among the rights of the People collectively (the State), the authority of each specific school, and the reasonable expectations of families. Their designs, formally presented orally and in written form to us and to some outsiders whom we had persuaded to be jurors, largely reflected a new balance of authority between central government, local communities, and families.

Who had the right to decide what is to be in the mind of each child was, for most of these college undergraduates, a question of fundamental importance. For them, centralized authority had neither all the answers nor the right to impose its own. It was not just ECS's experts and active politicians who sensed much wrong with our inherited top-down system of public schools.

Order and Authority

The 1893 Committee of Ten, Boston's Superintendent Gillis with his 1956 systemwide day-by-day directives to teachers, and the Federal No Child Left Behind Education Act of 2001 all reflect a belief in the need for order in schooling that arises from a detailed, uniform, imposed set of goals and procedures. All thereby tacitly reflected limited trust in school-level professionals to make not only major decisions but most minor ones as well.

There is irony here.

As with most professional work, the quality of a school is no better than the quality—the *authority*—of its on-the-line professionals, its teachers and administrators.

Most strong people only take and stay in jobs that entrust them with important things. That is, they—the Micheles, Edythes, and Phils of the world—expect to be free to exert their professional authority in ways they judge best serve their particular students at a particular time.

The more that higher authorities impose standardized procedures and demand that school-level people adhere to them, especially when these procedures have demonstrably limited merit in their particular situations, the greater is the likelihood that strong people will not join the profession or, if already in it, stay in the work but a short time—Peace Corps volunteer–like—even when the allure of working with children is an extraordinarily powerful one.

Learning and teaching is inescapably messy work. Adolescents especially are often volatile, changing before our eyes, testing their own freedoms, learning about life at every turn but often not in the ways we desire for them, understandably myopic (many think that life is no more or less than what they personally are experiencing). They do not pigeonhole. Ordering their lives with standardized procedures is a Procrustean bed: it fits some, but those it does not fit suffer.

Thus the more the system dictates, Superintendent Gillis–style, the greater the likelihood that the school will be mediocre, even harmful to some children, and unable to attract and hold a full complement of able staff. There rests the irony.

At the same time there has to be *order,* at the least in the sense that good schooling is made available to all young citizens wherever and in what conditions they live, and that the People generally are protected from incompetent, cruel, or corrupt school staff.

It is at this point that *authority* and *order* intertwine. Public schools must have authoritative staff, and the People need an orderly, universal system of schools.

Again, and as I have outlined in Chapter Two, an argument can be made for harmonious authority, a balance among the state, the school, and the family. A further argument can be made that such an arrangement is an example of admirable order—which brings us, perhaps oddly, back to football.

The state would set the key rules—yea, the *standardized* rules—providing the irreducible minimum of direction and inspection. It would provide for referees—inspectors to assure that these key governing rules are met. If the rules appeared to be egregiously ignored, the state could insist on timely changes.

To the maximum practical degree, schools should vary and families should have choice among them. The conviction that there is One Best School for all children should be replaced with the conviction that there should be One Best School for each individual child. Even as all schools (teams) share common goals (winning) and common overarching rules, no single school/team is likely or should be expected to be exactly like every other.

Money should follow the child (player), to each what is needed.

Order for strong education in a free society reflects an articulated, equitable, and richly varied system of schools, one where accountability is balanced between parental choice and state supervision, with a tilt toward the former.

The easy standardization genially reflected by Superintendent Gillis's boast is a recipe for disaster. And standardization of compulsory public education merely for the convenience of for-profit education businesses—as reflected by the exasperated plea of the Kennedy School speaker—is outrageous.

The sports metaphor works at least part way: competition within an accepted and refereed framework with local variety, each place seeking its own genius and gathering its own supporters.

Steve Sorota would understand both the aptness of the metaphor and its serious limitations. He accepted the order, and he gloried in his substantial freedom to work within it. Fortunately, Steve never knew that I too had been a football coach, for one year only, with middle school boys. Alas, we lost every game.

4   Horace Compromised

Horace Smith, a devoted high school English teacher, is my friend.

After observing him for twenty years, I believe that I know him well. Actually, he does not exist. He is a composite figure, an amalgam drawn of fine secondary school teachers whom I have observed and to whom I have listened over the past two decades. He is at once young and older, male and female, of every race, a blustering city teacher, an ingenious country teacher, a suburban teacher with kindly eyes that can stare down any inappropriately aggressive parent, a quiet person, a noisily colorful person, and more. I have listened to Horace carefully, admiringly, straining out of his words pride, frustration, exhilaration, embarrassed cynicism, passionate anger, and a deep love of kids and ideas.

I have observed and heard many less-devoted school folk as well—whiners, finger-pointers, malingerers, the holier-than-thou-types who put down their colleagues, people who yell at kids with an impatient rage that bespeaks their disinterest in, even loathing of, the youngsters they presumably serve, people who have no idea what scholarship is or exhibit any interest in finding out.

Yet it is Horace who sticks most firmly in my mind. He represents the dignity, principle, and devotion of the best of the American high school teaching force. The future of American education, I believe, rests more on his shoulders than on those of anyone else.

I had the opportunity of meeting Horace due to a large inquiry into American secondary schools that a group of us launched in 1981.[1] The Study of High Schools, as we called it, had three overlapping parts.

At its center was a detailed examination of fifteen varied high schools—rural, suburban, urban, public and private, small and large—sited in Massachusetts, Alabama, Ohio, Colorado, and California. Teams led by Arthur Powell, Eleanor Farrar, and David K. Cohen systematically observed these places over eighteen months. Their summary and analysis appeared in 1985 as *The Shopping Mall High School: Winners and Losers in the Educational Marketplace*.[2] Their central finding was reflected in their title: high school is a sorting system camouflaged as a school with many options in which some get ahead in the educational steeplechase and others do not. Most high schools are, thus, not consistently singular; they contain quite clearly, if usually undisclosed, sub-schools ("shops" of varying reputation and quality within the mall) that tend to follow racial and social class lines. Powell, Farrar, and Cohen detailed this complex, revealing, and persuasive perception.

Alongside this team stood the historian Robert Hampel, who looked carefully at the most recent decades of secondary school development. His findings appeared in 1986 as *The Last Little Citadel: American High Schools since 1940*.[3] Hampel explained that his title arose from the "1944 image for the high school belonging to the educator George Stoddard. His vision was of a secondary school of taste and intellect, a bastion against a rising sea of vulgarity and cant, a place for the last shot many young people would have at an education to prepare them for a difficult, often hostile world."[4] Hampel shows how this image was illusory; the high schools emerging after the Second World War were, for good or ill, more egalitarian, raucous, and politicized than what Stoddard had desired. The image of "citadel," still harbored today by many politically powerful Americans, was by 1980 a dream, and getting ever more so.

My task in the Study was to canvass carefully what my colleagues were unearthing and to visit, as quickly as feasible, a wide variety of schools across this country and, as it turned out, in southeastern Australia as well. I was not looking for answers to particular questions as much as I was looking for questions to ask.

My membership in the National Association of Secondary School Principals opened many doors, and I was generously welcomed in schools from California to Massachusetts, from Louisiana to Nebraska and Illinois. I watched and listened and took notes, as inconspicuously as possible. Each night I would retreat to a hotel room and dictate everything I could remember, of both specific conversations and observations and my take on what they appeared to tell me; the notes were transcribed back home and filed in four stuffed loose-leaf notebooks. From these sources, as well as from my colleagues' projects, I was to craft a "general readership" book. After several false starts, my Houghton Mifflin editor, Austin Olney, told me to relax, start over, and develop a narrative thread. For this I needed a central character and thereby met Horace Smith.[5]

What I learned from Horace was of his need to cut corners, to make a stream of little concessions in his teaching craft in order to meet the welter of obligations the system set him. It took time to extract this confession from him. He was skeptical of "outsiders" (my decade at privileged Phillips Academy gave me scant cover) and was damned if he was to be seen as a grumbler. Yet as we gradually connected, his sadness inevitably emerged. Horace could not meet the standard that he had set for himself. He was forced to compromise. It ate at him.

Good people are asked to do important things in settings ill designed for that purpose: This was a core finding in the High School Study, and for me it became a consuming issue. I was encouraged by the funders of the Study and others to move next to remedies. The result was the Coalition of Essential Schools, based, during its first decade, at Brown University in Providence, Rhode Island, where I went to teach in 1984.[6]

In the search for a "remedy," the first temptation was to go at once to structure—how the school day was to be organized, what the curriculum and assessments would be, and more—in essence a detailed Plan to Be Disseminated, Put Into Place, and Professionally Developed For. However, Horace was impatient with such a familiar but superficially rational approach as it denied the possibility of finding and then riding the special genius to be found in his and every other particular community. A uniform Plan might suit his place well in theory, but if the people who were going to live that plan were not part of its conception and if it did not reflect the best of their setting, then it would fail, if not at first then in the long run.

Horace had already lived through enough well-intended from-the-top-down mandates fueled by "professional development" from school of education circuit riders to be teetering on the edge of cynical stubbornness. Once again, when he heard of my new effort, he assumed that in due course "The Experts Will Arrive To Help Me By Telling Me In Detail How To Do My Job." The disrespect thereby signaled to him and to the best of his colleagues was palpable.

At the same time, to expect that all professional wisdom will arise locally is equally wrong-headed. A balance might emerge, I believed, by articulating what I and others on the Study staff believed to be core elements informing all of those schools we especially admired and by joining together schools that wished to use these principles as guideposts for their local reform, each in the way that promised the greatest success on its own turf. We at Brown would regularly gather staff from these schools for the exchange of their stories, and from these stories we would learn what worth resided in "reform" of this kind.

When I went on the publisher's circuit hawking the release of *Horace's Compromise*, I set these principles before many audiences of school people, and from these gatherings the first nibbles of interest emerged. There were nine principles in all.

Several were superficially banal in their obviousness: *The school should focus on helping young people use their minds well. The school's goals should apply to all students.*

Three were, by practical necessity, quite specific. If we had not asserted them so, they would have had no force: *No teacher should have more than* eighty *students. Essential schools should not attempt to provide an unrealistically wide range of academic, vocational, extracurricular, and social services. Less is more.*

A crucial principle that rolled its import back across the entire school had to do with assessment: *The diploma should be awarded upon a successful final demonstration of mastery for graduation—an "exhibition"—however long it took, whatever the age of the student.*

One had substantial ramifications for classes where the students traditionally sat and the teachers talked: *The governing practical metaphor of the school should be student-as-worker, rather than the more familiar teacher-as-deliverer-of-instructional-services.* Teaching would arise more from a curriculum of questions than a curriculum of answers; the point was to develop the habit of learning well and deeply on one's own. Teaching would therefore emphasize *coaching*, provoking students to understand what is before them and whetting their appetites for more—even if this resulted in less "coverage." Better to grasp a few essentially important things well than to skim over complexity.

Some were as necessarily vague as they were essential, for example: *The tone of the school should explicitly and self-consciously stress values of unanxious expectation ("I won't threaten you but I expect much of you"), of trust (until abused), and of decency (the values of fairness, generosity, and tolerance).*

Even as most were cast as provocations and in no way prescribed detailed universal practices, all were to hang together. We discouraged cherry pickers as we believed that, while some principles were politically easier to adopt than others were, all had to be addressed simultaneously.

In *Horace's Compromise* I followed these principles with five "imperatives for better schools":

1. Give room to teachers and students to work and learn in their own, appropriate ways.
2. Insist that students clearly exhibit mastery of their school work.
3. Get the incentives right, for students and for teachers.
4. Focus the students' work on the use of their minds.
5. Keep the structure simple and thus flexible.[7]

I received few sharp criticisms about the merit of these principles and imperatives; most people across education's ideological spectrum appeared to acknowledge their merit, indeed their common sense. I was, however, troubled by the unexpected inertia of those with whom I talked. "Nice ideas," I was told. "But we can't take them seriously." "Why not?" I would ask. "We just couldn't."

Nonetheless, a small band of like-minded colleagues did emerge. Dennis Littky, the principal of a small, desperately poor high school in rural New Hampshire, was the first to call. Judy Codding, the principal of a wealthy suburban high school in Bronxville, New York, got in touch. Clint Vickers, the head of a small private school in Brooklyn, called: would we consider an independent school in our effort? Deborah Meier, a Kindergarten teacher and progressive founder of inner-city elementary schools in New York, made contact: could I support her start of a secondary school in East Harlem? A small Catholic girls' school in Rhode Island, St Xavier's Academy, asked to be included. Via my sister Caroline Cochran in Baltimore came an inquiry from Samuel Billups, the principal of that city's Walbrook High School: could we help him start a small Essential school within his large high school? A school board member from Portland, Maine, called: could we help the new principal of Portland High School, Barbara Anderson, turn her school around?

From Laredo, Texas, came another private school inquiry: Charlie Como asked whether his small United Day School on the border between the United States and Mexico might be an Essential school. A group of teachers in Houston, Texas's Westbury High School had read *Horace's Compromise* and formed a supper-and-discussion group ("Horace's Company," they called themselves) about its ideas; the principal, Tom Davis, heard of the talk and expressed strong interest: would I help them start a small school within their big, sprawling, troubled school? Two Andover alumni in Fort Worth, Texas, were in touch: would I help in the creation of a small school within R. L. Paschal Senior High School? Closer to home—a few blocks down the street from our Brown offices—the principal of Hope High School, Paul Gounaris, inquired: what about an Essential school neighbor? And more. By 1985 we had a dozen varied, lively schools engaged. By the end of the decade there were hundreds involved.

These principals and the teachers from these schools and others gathered often to compare notes and counsel one another. Those in large city high schools who elected to create from scratch small Essential schools that drew volunteer faculty and students from within their buildings moved ahead more readily than those that tried to turn their entire institutions at once. Indeed, the Essential principle of "knowing the students well" seemed unattainable in the teeming crowds of adolescents found in large high schools.

Institutional self-satisfaction in wealthy schools smothered thoughts of change. For them, and for their constituencies, good enough appeared to be good enough, even though what was considered "good" was for many students threadbare. Nonetheless, even a suggestion of improvement assaulted their dignity.

As the effort grew I saw Horace in a new and constructive light: an active Reformer (although he would dismiss that loaded designation as a pretension) rather than as a mildly cynical, albeit ever loving, critic of his place of work. Around my university duties I continued to travel, listen, and watch, this time in those places that were struggling to improve their schools. I saw patterns in the work at those places and spun the most positive of their stories into another book, *Horace's School*, using the device of a fictional faculty committee charged with redesign, highlighting what had given all of the Essential schools their most demanding task, the construction of the Exhibitions for graduation.[8] Horace Smith was the lead character in that fictional Franklin High School.

In 1988, the Coalition's effort received a major boost with the offer of an anonymous donor to ally our effort with that at the Education Commission of the States, thereby connecting our work with that on policy and system practice. Frank Newman, the President of ECS, had deep Brown connections, and Howard Swearer, the university's President, encouraged us. After several hilarious sessions (policy folk and school folk—the macro and the micro—have not a great deal in common) at ECS's headquarters in Denver, Colorado, we settled on an apt slogan for our collective work: "From the schoolhouse to the statehouse." Our agreed-upon task was to reverse at least some of the current of policy influence, traditionally from "the top" down, now to include imperatives that seemed essential to Horace Smith. We titled our effort Re:Learning, a title with a coy double meaning for both school and policy communities.

Governors got aboard, some (I later realized) merely for the money and the publicity. Others, however, pushed their state authorities to lighten up regulation and attend to the ideas of sensible, veteran school-level people. Roy Roemer of Colorado, Bill Clinton of Arkansas, John Ashcroft of Missouri, Evan Bayh of Indiana, Michael Castle of Delaware, Gary Carothers of New Mexico, and Carroll Campbell of South Carolina were among those involved. The effect at the grass roots was encouraging; the numbers of schools pushing to reshape themselves grew. Blessing from the top clearly helped. The initiative soon included elementary schools, and a version of the Common Principles appropriate to their calling evolved. I wrote of all this at century's end in *Horace's Hope: What Works for the American High School,* with an extended appendix prepared by Margaret M. MacMullen on the emerging national research data on Essential schools' progress.[9]

For a variety of reasons (few arising, however, from Horace's particular painful compromises), governors across the country collectively had become ever more interested in serious school reform, culminating in their Charlottesville Summit meeting in 1989 with President George H. W. Bush to launch a crusade of national reform. Education was now held once again to be "in crisis," and governments at every level were importuned to address it. That attitude spread. For me personally the capstone of all this heady national activity was the extraordinary $500 million challenge for school reform that the philanthropist Walter Annenberg offered to the nation, an initiative helped into being by Brown's then-President, Vartan Gregorian, with the assistance of his Brown-based university colleagues.

Horace, alas, got lost in all of this. The abrupt arrival of school reform on the national stage energized powers up and down the education system. Horace's school was now the object of attention, and advantages, monetary and political, accrued from it. But authority flowed increasingly upward, away from his beloved Franklin High School and its community's sense of what was wrong and what should be done about it, to the districts, then to the states, and eventually to the Federal government. Little shared authority emerged from all this. What counted, apparently, was something vague called "policy."

Horace was right about the need for reform, but now he was to be the agent for centralized government's standardized remedies rather than the driver of those that he and his local colleagues felt were of greatest moment. Headlong-mandated homogeneity descended on American public education, this symbolized by standardized testing and the curricula that drove it. Higher, apparently, was wiser. "Local control" was deemed a failure—even as some extraordinarily effective schools, such as Deborah Meier's Central Park East Secondary School in New York City, Dennis Littky's Thayer High School in New Hampshire, Sam Billups's Walbrook Essential High School in Baltimore, the Essential school within Fort Worth's R. L. Paschal Senior High School, and others had broken dramatically and successfully away from the hierarchy's conventional patterns and, given the remarkable success of the graduates of these schools, provided a promising new direction. But no; these schools and those like them were expected to stop what they were doing and prepare for the promised torrent of detailed standardized curriculum frameworks and testing.

Something had to be done, political leaders dictated; the states and the Feds had to do it, and what was done was not invigoration and stronger incentives for bold local initiative but, rather, top-down direction. That direction assumed that the system as it existed would remain largely in place, leaving all of Horace's compromises intact, and at the same time shuffling aside, with little comment, questions of authority, of fairness, of equity, of just who in our democracy has the power to shape each child's mind.

Silences

I often speak with school system administrators of Horace's compromises, and almost always do they mention, with pride, the Horaces on their faculties. They do not mention his job obligations, however, those 120 kids he sees in snippets of time most days in class.

Horace cannot teach well the 120 students the system assigns him, I tell my administrator friends, particularly if those 120 are shuffled at the end of each semester. Horace can "deliver" stuff. But teach it, in any deep sense? *No,* my friends sheepishly reply.

Most people do not learn important things in rushed forty-seven-minute chunks of time, with the subject of discussion changed hourly, I argued. *Yes,* the administrators replied. *We agree. That's a recipe for intellectual confusion.* So, why organize that way? *How else are we going to get everything in?* Narrow the program. *We can't do that.*

The formal assessments used in the high schools tell us something but hardly everything about the students, I continue. To use the scores arising from those assessments alone as the only benchmark of a student's qualifications and performance is both misleading and unfair. *Yes, that is so. But we have to rank the kids somehow.* But your rankings are likely to be profoundly flawed. *Yes. But it is the best we can do.* Some kids get hurt in the process. *Yes, some do.* More than a few? *Yes, more than a few. The system stinks.* So why don't you insist that it be changed? *Come on. You've got to be kidding . . . no one's going to change the system.*

I persist. Adolescents develop in fits and starts, physically and intellectually. Their chronological age tells us something but not everything. Age grading then makes little organizational sense. *Yes. You are right.* So why use it? *Kids and their parents expect graduation when the student is about* eighteen, *not before and not afterward.* So, when all is said and done, high school is far more a rite of passage than a place to learn to use your mind and heart well. *I suppose you are right.*

You have what most consider to be an excellent high school, I say. *Yes, ours is a good school, a Blue Ribbon school. The teachers work hard and the kids do too.* All of them? *No, not all of them.* Why not all of them? *Get real. Some kids don't want to learn.* I agree. But does letting them simply go through the motions of attending school help anyone? *No.*

Some critics say that your schools' fine reputations rest almost wholly on the performance—academically, athletically, and artistically—of a highly visible minority of the students. *Well, perhaps they do. We don't like to think of it that way.* If you ever did accept the critics' observation, what could you do to spread the "excellence" over more students? *There is not much that we could do without more money or a big change in priorities for the school. The Board of Education would not stand for it.* Come on, I protest. Your school has a nationally typical fourteen to one student to staff ratio. What do you mean that you have little wiggle room? *The contract and regulation so fixes the jobs that any change is barely possible.* Still, have you at least tried to loosen all this up, even raised the question? *No.*

Why? *They, the Board, the superintendent, the union leaders, do not want to rock the boat. If their own kids are in our school, they are the high-visibility ones. We make sure that we take good care of them. And those Board members without kids in school just want peace, winning teams, and a bare-bones budget. They hate all those special-interest mandates too. They complain that these soak up the money that should be shared by all students.*

So, you don't suggest big changes? *No. The Boards and the communities are satisfied with how things are. Or, perhaps, they are scared that something new will make things worse. Sure, they rant and rave, but ultimately they go along with what we have.* Do you lose kids to private schools and Charter schools? *Yes. We wish they didn't exist, especially Charter schools. They hurt. We cannot compete.* Why? Some of the private schools, especially the Catholic ones, have smaller per-pupil funding than you do, and the Charter schools match you dollar for dollar, by law. *They don't have the restraints that we have.* Really? The Charter schools have similar requirements for Special Needs and all that. *Yes, but it is different.* Why different? *Our Boards like us just about the way we are. To change much would create all sorts of political problems. . . . We have pride, you know. Why do you keep badgering us? I hope the Boards don't hear all this.* You mean that you can't level with them on what you really want and know that you need to do? *No, they do not want to hear anything like that.*

And so the silence starts with educators, and their professional organizations, who believe that they cannot be insistent truth-tellers, despite decades of careful research that illumines the serious problems they face daily, such studies as those by James Coleman, John Goodlad, Laurence Steinberg, Seymour Sarason, Mihalyi Csikszent-mihalyi, and scores of others, and of stories that put faces on those problems, sometimes with devastating (as well as often loving) directness, as in Jonathan Kozol's 1991 account of children in America's schools, *Savage Inequalities*, Samuel Freedman's 1990 chronicle of a year at New York City's Seward Park High School, *Small Victories*, H. G. Bissinger's *Friday Night Lights* (also from 1990, about "a town, a team," and the high school housing those football players), Frank McCourt's often hilarious *'Tis* and Mark Edmundson's 2002 book, *Teacher*, about one radiantly effective instructor at the high school in Medford, Massachusetts.[10]

The silence continues in the policy community. Policy makers largely focus on the effectiveness, or lack thereof, of the schools as they are (not as they might be), primarily using such data as known-to-be-wobbly scores on standardized tests as their primary, sometimes only, measure of performance. School objectives like "good citizenship" are articulated but rarely addressed save at the organizational margins ("Does the school have a Service Learning program?" as though mere presence of such an activity denoted success with school and student citizenship). The breathtaking inequities across the public and private school systems are periodically recognized and pressed by such scholars as Gary Orfield of the Harvard Civil Rights Project and Marian Wright Edelman of the Children's Defense Fund but as a matter of policy remain carefully off to the side, nibbled at on technical terms, treated as hot potatoes, rarely on the insistent agendas of state legislatures and their consultants. And the extraordinary intellectual and emotional influences on young citizens' learning beyond the walls of schools, on the street, at jobs, absorbing the media's fare are a topic almost totally divorced from discussions of "education."

The silence extends to the very heart of democracy, with remarkably little serious consideration, save at the frustrated, noisy margins, about just who has the right—the democratic authority—to decide where a child must attend school, to direct how the resources of that school are to be deployed, and—most importantly—to insist upon the furniture and discipline of that child's mind.

In due course, the silence reaches the practicalities of school operation and the need and expectation for order, "order" represented as low-cost standardization, this accepted with barely a whimper of challenge.

The existence of all these silences is itself a puzzle. Why is it so, especially when the issues before Americans are so clear and the evidence of the costs to the society so persuasive?

Of course, such "silences" are not unique to education. Humans' overuse of fossil fuels, global inequities, and unrestrained population growth, for example, are much larger and equally transparent matters. For most Americans, including most political leaders, however, they are at once recognized and invisible issues, abstractions and thus not yet distractions in daily life, ones easily put out of mind, put off for another day.

Contrarily, Horace's necessary but unworthy compromises are neither abstract nor difficult to appreciate and measure. Simple arithmetic will do: Horace has 120 senior high school students. If he wants each of them to produce two pieces of substantial writing each week, and if reading and writing comments on each paper takes him, on average, a total of five minutes, that results in four hours of "grading papers" every weeknight all year long, an utterly impossible task, and this on top of preparing his classes and keeping up with his discipline. If we really care about high standards in English, how can we continue smothering Horace with legions of students?

Few serious business enterprises, save those expecting only mindless labor, break up their intellectual work into snippets of time, arranged in no intellectually coherent order. If this is so, why do we think that such practice makes sense for schools?

The differences in provision for schooling represented in the Bronx and in nearby Bronxville, New York; for schooling in Massachusetts' Andover Public Schools, Phillips Academy, and immediately adjacent Lawrence Public Schools; for public schooling in Lake Forest and Chicago, Illinois, Beverly Hills and Compton, California, are stark, visible, and widespread. Do these differences properly represent the just and fair society that we say we are? If not, why don't all of us—not just the peripheral Greek chorus of predictably marginalized "special interest groups"—say so, loudly and persistently?

The painful, embarrassing inertia persists.

Why?

There must be reasons for these persistent silences. Five are worth considering.

One may simply be that the American system of schooling allows financially secure and thus politically influential families to opt out of schools that they dislike, usually by means of relatively well financed suburban public schools and private schools. The rich thereby feel no fire directly beneath their feet. Their school politics, full as they may be of good intentions and stirring calls for accountability, reflect that disengagement. There is little direct motivation for these politically influential people to raise awkward questions about the system of schooling as a whole. We are doing all right, they quietly agree. Let sleeping dogs lie.

A second reason surely lies in expense. The polity knows that American education is sputtering—enough "commission" reports have told them that—but they also know that making consequential changes to the operation of the system could take a great deal of money and even more political capital. Better, it seems, to go the public relations route of jawboning, praising some and humiliating others, or to focus primarily on "outcomes," all the while expecting the schools to remain financially and organizationally as they are but now suffering threats arising solely from test scores.

A third reason rises from the intricate complexity of school programs, especially those of secondary schools. So many separated programs are stuffed into too little space and time, each protected by its own dignities, politically well-wired supporters, and Byzantine regulation, that even to fiddle with much of it usually provokes a small war. To add or subtract something substantial creates a major conflagration. Better to tinker, hoping that gradual tidal motions will wash out the less important bits of the school schedule and provide a tiny bit of room for the necessary new.[11]

A fourth reason may be fear. Watch the faces of upper-middle-class Americans when suddenly confronted, say on a subway platform, by a large gathering of noisy adolescents and sense the apprehension. Too many of us are afraid of our children (especially those who do not look like us), and we want others to insist on orderliness and to teach order—and to keep the kids invisible in the process. Silence masks our fear of the young. If we refuse to hear their legitimate complaints, we can live with limited obligations to them.

The fear bites deeper, however, when we recall the hopes for all Americans that we frequently express. In his recent book *The American Dream*, Jim Cullen cites Abraham Lincoln as he addressed a special session of the Congress on July 4, 1861, about the outbreak of the Civil War, a conflict that the president believed to be "a Peoples' contest." The "form and substance of government," Lincoln said, has as the "leading object . . . to elevate the condition of men—to lift artificial weights from their shoulders—to clear the paths of laudable pursuit for all— to afford all, an unfettered start, and a fair chance, in the race of life."[12]

An unfettered start . . . A fair chance in the race of life . . . Government's leading object . . . to elevate the Peoples' condition.

Such sentiments still ring true to many Americans. As Cullen implies, however, deep down we know that the school systems and analogous institutions that we have inherited—well intentioned and dutifully managed though they may be—dramatically fail to meet that mid-nineteenth-century test.

We know that the rich get the better scores and the poor get the compromises. When we once admit to ourselves that reality, the fear sets in. Have we lost that Dream? If so, what should we do? What, as a practical and political matter, *can* we do?

The lack of an easy answer eats at us, paralyzing our voices.

A final explanation of the silences is personally painful, because of my professional history as a Professor of Education: what saddens and embarrasses me has been the remarkable inattention to these silences by the universities, especially their Schools of Education. Some of the rhetoric is there, but remarkably little decisive action.

Most Education schools are organized as shadows of the architecture of the existing system, Horace's many compromises and all, including the plethora of largely unconnected and coordinated activities and subjects. In Schools of Education, save for a few introductory courses, undergraduate and graduate students preparing to be secondary school professionals work in one or another of these intellectually confined domains. Although most Education programs have a few courses in "philosophy" and in "secondary education," places where fundamental rethinking of the enterprise might happen, these generally are peripheral electives disconnected from the bread-and-butter certification programs.

The brass ring for graduate students and professors alike is certification in one's technical specialty and induction into its professional groups, with an impetus to leave classroom work and get into research, management, or consulting. The signal sent to the newcomers thereby is clear: your career needs to start down a familiar, well-traveled road. Call it the system, the way we do things. Accept it, and figure out how to do the best within it, making the fewest possible compromises. Join the appropriate Washington area–headquartered professional association to stay ever more focused on—and to rise within—your specialty. With hard work and luck, you can soon leave the daily, unrelenting grind of a high school classroom and enter the somewhat more rational (and likely better paid) world of Education school teaching, research, and consulting. If you aspire to lead an institution made up of several specialties, to become a high school principal, perhaps, focus on skills of management, of "leadership" of what exists—an institution consisting of the sum of independently defined and endorsed parts. Do not contemplate rocking any important boats.

In most universities, there appears to be little room, much less initiative, for challenge to this professional mindset. Some professors have written powerfully about the inadequacies of the system—most call them "radicals," on either the Left or the Right—and have lively coteries of followers, but their mother institutions show little effect of their arguments. The momentum of the old ways is extraordinary. The fact that the existing secondary school system is itself "radical" — in the sense that it fails to meet obvious, commonsense conditions for learning—makes a charge of extremism bizarre.

Not surprisingly, few major school reform efforts over the past five decades have emerged from Education schools. The curriculum redesign initiatives of the late 1950s and 1960s disproportionately came from outside professional education, from places like MIT with the work of Jerrold Zacharias, Jerome Wiesner, and their colleagues.[13] Paideia emerged from Mortimer Adler at the independent Institute for Philosophical Research in Chicago. Few of the energetic 1980s–90s school reform models arose from Education schools. Dr. James Comer's work emerged at the Yale Medical School. The Coalition of Essential Schools was birthed in a tiny education department in a liberal arts university. Core Knowledge was started by E. D. Hirsch, a Professor of English at the University of Virginia, Accelerated schools by an economist nominally at Stanford's School of Education, and America's Choice from the not-for-profit National Center on Education and the Economy. Schools of Education have joined in at later points, but they were rarely the engines of the new ideas or the seedbeds for more and better efforts.

There appears to be little incentive in these Schools for aggressively original, sustained, comprehensive *invention*. Analysis and assessment of the status quo, largely dependent on statistics, are King. There is nothing wrong with analysis and measurement, but if they dominate the institutional culture one ends with Education Schools that are focused more on the techniques of autopsy than with the creation of

new life, surer of tinkering with the accepted rather than risking something new. The current fascination with—and profound abuse of—
standardized testing is reason enough for the universities to take stock,
and the lack of incentives for new creation, including the time necessary
for these inventions to find their feet before the unsmiling analysts
move in, is saddening.

A massive failure of imagination resides here, a curious and embarrassing condition in what are otherwise powerful universities, places
that have been critical shapers of priorities and practice in other fields.
There is also a massive failure of courage on the parts of university
presidents on the issue of intellectual freedom. If the state insisted on
specifying their universities' curricula, teaching, and assessment with
the same fervor that has been imposed on public schools, the howls
about the need for their teachers' academic freedom and for independence from intrusive political incursion would be instantaneous, sustained, and noisy. Not so with the secondary schools. Apparently the
differences between the minds of twelfth graders and those of thirteenth
graders and the dignity of their teachers are so great that detailed political direction of the learning of the former and the academic freedom
for the latter is fully justified. So the spokespeople at the universities
remain silent, and the political establishment assumes that such silence
means acquiescence, even endorsement.

The silences, so obvious and so pressing, seem ever harder to fill.
For any one of us to expect that filling to be carried solely on the
shoulders of grassroots school people and parents alone, this in the
teeth of the self-protective arguments (or silences) of the mandarins
of the "system," is naive.

Ambiguous Moments

In his essay on education in early American society cited in the first chapter of this book, the historian Bernard Bailyn used the metaphor of
"soft, ambiguous moments" when the connections between institutions

and the functions they are meant to perform became detached, strained, confused, and uncertain. Such "moments," Bailyn argued, can be "moments of true origination."[14]

At first this seems a paradox: confusion and uncertainty are the fuel for imaginative change? On reflection, the argument makes sense. Wise democratic societies learn—slowly, but they learn—from the expensive, disordering disjunctions between activities shaped by an earlier, different context and the insistent needs of the present. The process of adaptation and invention can be tortuous, painful, and prone to error, as Americans are currently experiencing with their educational system. The evidence of its inadequacy has turned from a trickle to a torrent. America, therefore, may be at such an "ambiguous moment," a time where nothing seems to work well, where there is finger-pointing, name-calling, frustration, threat, but little legitimate progress.

Kicking a broken horse, obviously, cannot make it run faster. Although democratic societies may have to do some kicking before they are ready to accept the fact that the race they wish to run may require a different approach, perhaps the moment of acceptance has arrived for education.

Maybe our times are not yet exactly "soft," but they are clearly ambiguous, uncertain, and fraught with tension. Let us take heart from the existence of the ambiguity, even as we regret that what we call School, designed in the late nineteenth century, cannot run well any longer.

Requiescat in Pacem. Now let us start anew.

Epilogue: Dodging Our Duty

Memories of sweaty palms in a 1946 Latin class taught by Joe Barrell mingle at the end of my career with equally intense images.

In the spring of 2003 I attended a conference involving prominent Massachusetts opinion makers who were generally labeled "neoconservatives," people similar to those in the 1960s who had been tagged as "liberal Republicans" but who in our time have been right-of-center, powerful advocates for systemic state school reform. Few of the speakers had any personal experience in high school work but all spoke with the confidence of people who felt that their message was correct, that they had gained the confidence of the public, and that their agenda had become the mainspring of state policy.

I agreed with that latter assessment. The centralized standards-setting-testing-rewards-and-punishments strategy had powerful allies in Massachusetts, from a succession of Republican governors through a conservative Democrat state legislature to the organized business community and the most influential newspapers, the *Boston Globe* and *Boston Herald*. Academia went along with it. "Standards-based reform" was the law of the state. The not-so-tacit assumption was that earlier standards had been too low or, in effect, nonexistent. There was much truth in that assumption. Some schools needed a vigorous shove.

I did not begrudge these leaders their sense of success. At the same time, I was disheartened by the willingness of these supposedly conservative, and thus likely "small government" advocates, to encourage political authorities far from the classrooms to decide what will be taught. I can live with general state outlines for effective literacy and numeracy. The details of history, literature, the arts, and science, however, by their very nature will always be matters about which reasonable citizens and scholars can and should disagree. To leave the resolution of that dispute to people far from those directly affected strikes me as excessive centralization in a democracy. I was getting regretfully accustomed to that peculiar philosophical inconsistency, however.

Most troubling to me was the sense that my neoconservative acquaintances had missed many of the most important parts of the problem they wished to solve and were stunningly unimaginative and conventional in their primary remedies to the state system's besetment. Their braggadocio masked costly ignorance. I agreed with their ends. I disagreed with many, if not all, of their means.

The speakers' constant reference to "data-driven policy" and "research," with the assumption that these drove their reform agenda, was especially irritating.

Data emerging from forty years of research, the most sophisticated of them knew, strongly suggest that no child's accomplishment can be accurately and fairly assessed by a single test. Nonetheless, a single score on a standardized test, the speakers agreed, served to sort out these children and their schools.[1]

Most of the speakers at the conference, I knew, would be outraged if their own upper-middle-class children were so cavalierly pigeonholed or their favored schools so brusquely dismissed. I was reminded of this double standard while serving recently on an admissions committee at the Harvard Graduate School of Education. We examined piles of applicants' credentials, including test scores. We acknowledged the scores' importance but concentrated much of our energy on other records—references, statements of purpose, evidence of persistence and imagination, social class and national background. We made our decisions, often with split votes, on the basis of judgments informed by varied information—that is, relevant "data." Nonetheless, many of us in our own research continue to make judgments about the "success" and "failure" of children and schools on the basis of test scores alone. "But that's all we have to work with," some of us say. That is, of course, an embarrassing cop-out.

Forty years of careful data collection have shown that most "scores" correlate closely with social class. Nonetheless, virtually nothing was said at this conference about the possible meanings and implications of this finding, or even about narrowly defined "opportunity-to-learn standards"—arrangements in schools to provide all youngsters a fair, common academic playing field and for their teachers the conditions of work necessary to teach well. The findings of the massive James Coleman–led 1966 *Report on Equal Educational Opportunity* required by the Civil Rights Act of 1964 and the procession of similarly persuasive studies that followed upon it found little expression in early twenty-first-century policy.

Forty years of careful research have catalogued the inefficiencies and mindless overload of secondary school organization and operation. Nonetheless, the speakers assumed that all of that would remain, and tests would be imposed by "grade level" (that is, chronological age) and in utterly unconnected academic "subjects." There was nary a whisper of any reconstruction of the system and its schools on the basis of research. All was to remain much as it was, even though the findings of that research indicated profound flaws.

Largely absent in their remarks was the recognition, or even the possibility, that the *system,* that within which we were supposed to work harder—including the very way we define it—is palpably obsolete. The physical and pedagogical architecture, and the assumptions behind it, of my 1946 Pomfret classroom remains in place today. It was inefficient then, and it is inefficient now.

Imposing "standards," testing, and "privatizing" on a dysfunctional system of schools is not *re-form*, in the core meaning of that word. The "data" and "research" so warmly embraced at this conference were selective, cherry-picked for what was politically correct, unlikely to discomfit the existing power groups, and carrying no new costs.

However, to write off the priorities these leaders articulated as mere insincerity, political bludgeoning, and heedlessness is unfair. These people are far better than that, and they deserve applause for surfacing a complex and politically charged public policy area, one that has been artfully avoided by all too many leaders for all too many decades. To find sweeping fault in their efforts is to belittle the important fact that they have got the attention of the people on the inadequacy of the schools. That is a significant first step—but only that and no more.

What they might have said—indeed, should have said—on the basis of data arising from research is that we must start anew, very carefully, with an educating system—schools and much, much more —that reflects modern realities of the America of our time rather than those of Charles Eliot's time. We need to *invent*.

A good place to start would be to fill the silences, to focus on what "school" should be. The specific tasks, those that I have addressed in Chapter One ("Building") and Chapter Three ("Order"), are the easiest to imagine.

Accept the reality that the shape of formal schooling for adolescents may be substantially different than that for young children.

Define the deliberate education of adolescents as more than what takes place in a school building. "School" would no longer be "comprehensive"; "education" would be. Make maximum possible use of constructive agencies and arrangements beyond the school building. Where few exist, take a lead in energizing them.

Where necessary, be advocates for the students. Stay with them if they have no one else on whom to depend.

Define formal education in terms of each student's exhibited performance rather than services delivered on his or her behalf.

Design each youngster's educational program around his or her particular needs and potential. Know each child well. Accept diversity. Indeed, rejoice in it.

Make standardization a policy of last resort.

Finance schooling by a system of warrants that follow each adolescent child, scaled to reflect the wealth of his or her family. Relate these warrants to those provided for parallel social services.

Expect the state to set the terms and general rules for public provision for education, encouraging variety in the forms of that provision. Educators would design and operate the provided programs. Families would choose among providers; financial support for the provision would follow the child.

Reenergize and protect the public's interest and claim over the nation's mass communication systems.

More difficult will be filling the silences described in Chapter Two ("Authority"). Tolerating variety and trusting grassroots people are unfamiliar habits among Americans who exercise power (like the neoconservatives at my meeting), even when they face its necessity. Too many believe that authority has to be centralized and that only those who have power hold truth about structures and standards. Democracies are built on different assumptions, however, and require effort, restraint, and respect—qualities in too little abundance today.

Americans have run out the string on "school" as it has evolved over the past century. Tinkering with it, testing it, belittling it, pouring money into it as it is makes ever less sense. The painful work of reconstituting what we mean by "school" for adolescents is no longer avoidable.

Fortunately, there are some early, tentative, fragile representations of reconstitution—both physical and philosophical—that are cause for hope. Even though most are still more or less traditional "schools" and are largely at the margins of policy and practice, their approaches are promising.

Not surprisingly, most of these schools are only partway along the process of breaking with unpersuasive and wasteful traditional practice. Most, for example, still operate on a nine-month rather than a year-round calendar. Most are freestanding entities; few share space and programs with other congenial enterprises like public libraries and theaters, neighborhood service centers, or community colleges.

Some are no more complicated than five or six teachers within an existing large middle or high school who gain full responsibility for the work of, say, 130 students, with accountability being a combination of parental choice and independent inspection on terms agreed upon up front. Others are fully freestanding and authorized schools. There are dozens of small "spin-offs" from comprehensive high schools, some of long standing in such affluent suburbs as Brookline, Massachusetts, and Scarsdale, New York, as well as in inner cities.

Most are public schools. Some are private.

Most of these secondary schools are small, serving 150 to 400 students, most of whom arrive at age fourteen (traditional ninth graders) and some at age eleven (traditional seventh graders).

Some are in cities, some in suburbs and exurbia, some in places thinly populated. Some independent and Charter schools draw students from across wide geographic areas.

Most serve the full traditional functions of formal schooling and have authority to do so. Some are only "add-on" programs to traditional schools.

Most focus on core, traditional academic subjects: English, mathematics, science, history, government, foreign languages, and the arts, these often taught in combination. Most depend heavily on technology for library resources and other services unlikely to be available to new, financially lean schools.

Many require supervised and assessed out-of-school-based work like internships and paid part-time jobs.

Although most depend for some of their functioning on the voluntary efforts of the families they serve, few are fully integrated into their communities (in the historical manner, say, of some early twentieth-century Catholic parochial schools).

Most are schools of choice. Many admit their students, often by lottery, from among interested families. Most serve a fair complement of students with "special needs." Most disproportionately serve children from lower income families, providing them with choices generally available to families with substantial means.

Many have smaller per-pupil financial allotments than schools serving middle-class youngsters.

Some are performance driven; that is, the students progress on the basis of their exhibited academic and social performance. They graduate when they exhibit the mastery required for completion.

Most are resented, albeit tolerated, by traditional school authorities. Most depend on the state-level political support of a mix of often unusual political bedfellows, the "privatizing antigovernment conservatives" and the "antibureaucracy, pro-traditional-democracy liberals."

Some serve as the pivots for a variety of social service agencies, becoming in effect "community schools." None serving mostly lower income children rest (to my knowledge) in neighborhoods characterized by robust "social capital." They are thus only partially able to serve their children, trying as best they can to ameliorate the effects of poverty rather than being participants in a network of related services where the schools are but a part of a multifaceted community effort to eliminate the effects of hardship—the kind of collaborative effort that one finds in some (but hardly all) more affluent communities.

There are the dozens of small secondary schools of choice in New York City, experienced for almost a quarter century at battling city and state bureaucracies intent on getting them in line while graduating scores of kids who, by socioeconomic standards, would traditionally be very unlikely to graduate. They have their cousins in Chicago, Oakland, Seattle, and elsewhere.

Some spring from smaller communities but are spreading nationally, like the Met Schools, which originated first at Brown University's Annenberg Institute and then at the not-for-profit Big Picture Company in Providence, Rhode Island; the EdVisions schools, which emerged from the small, rural New Country School in Henderson, Minnesota; and High Tech High schools, which had their start in San Diego, California. A rapidly growing number are small autonomous schools lodged together in buildings that had earlier been large, centrally administered high schools, like the Julia Richman Educational Complex in New York, started over a decade ago as part of that city's Coalition Campus Project designed by Deborah Meier, Ann Cook, and their colleagues.[2]

Many are associated with the Coalition of Essential Schools and kindred reform organizations. Many are supported—and thereby protected—by private national foundations, notably the Bill and Melinda Gates Foundation and the Carnegie Corporation of New York. Federal moneys have been increasingly available. Increasing numbers are benefiting from the admirable *Breaking Ranks* and *Breaking Ranks II* reports of the National Association of Secondary School Principals, which recommend school-level practices akin to those I have described.[3]

Together these schools are best described as a "movement" rather than the outcome of an organized national strategy arising from a detailed business plan. They represent the coalescence of the convictions and experience of scores of determined school people and their friends, and the conversations among them are the mechanism by which worthy ideas and practices move.

In recent years, this movement has been powerfully helped by the existence of state or local Charter or Pilot schools laws, by means of which authorities have explicitly given running room—and not with just a wink—to people with the itch to try something new. Here I have had personal experience; the Francis W. Parker Charter Essential School in Devens, Massachusetts, of which Nancy and I were among the founders and for which we served as Acting co-Principals for a year, is one of these enterprises.

Many of these schools have received support from across the political spectrum—neoconservatives paradoxically supporting progressive places, populists supporting traditional programs, and everything in between. In many places there are a variety of educational initiatives working within a unified political environment that protects their right to be different. There is unity over the end and variety among the means.

In spite of this, the fight to keep these schools free of excessively standardized and politically motivated mandates persists. All of these schools—expressions of the disorder that so frightens many political authorities—are at risk.

To my eye, all of these schools, however under pressure, begin to address—if not yet fill—the "silences" that are the substance of this book. At the least they discomfort the guardians of the status quo. At best they are harbingers of fresh responses to our day's "soft, ambiguous moment" fraught with "confusion and uncertainty."

The Red Pencil's three silences are neither new nor misunderstood. They yet remain relative silences because too many of us—including the speakers at the Massachusetts conference I attended—dare not break them, as their implications, at least on a sustained, large scale, are too substantial to contemplate. To tackle them would require hard, expensive, and controversial work. They require a variety of approaches. Save at the obvious margins, therefore, there is unlikely to be a quick replacement for the early twentieth-century hierarchical system to which we cleave.

Most difficult for governments will be the leap from "school" to an arrangement that reflects both "school" and the conditions, hazards, and opportunities beyond school—the street, the media, work, family. Most of the programs that I admire are barely halfway toward that sort of comprehensiveness. The bureaucratic, political, financial, professional—and particularly the intellectual—barriers to going further are heroic. The social class barriers, the "surround," so compellingly described by careful researchers for half a century, stunt such leverage that these institutions have.

Rather than shouldering this task, too many of our political and educational leaders rest behind the traditional system, masking their lack of imagination with tough talk, dodging their duty.

That posture is understandable, if not admirable. Heading down a new road—a better way of casting adolescent education—will be difficult. Doing right by our children will require courage to think in new ways about learning in a democracy. We will need thick skins and stamina on a scale not seen on behalf of the education of young Americans since the first decades of the twentieth century.

It is a road worth taking. I wish that I had a second lifetime to join in the trek.

Acknowledgments

To acknowledge fully and specifically all those who influenced and helped during a professional lifetime would be impossible. I am indebted to hundreds of people, many of whom I mentioned in the foregoing pages.

None is more important than Nancy, my wife and (as is clear from this book) my closest professional colleague. We met as teenagers, and our academic and personal lives have been woven together ever since. Her influence on what I have here written is immense. Although she would usually preface an observation about some theory I was propounding with the briskly ironic "While I am *just a teacher . . .*" qualification, she cut to the quick on all matters educational. Her professional and parental career itself tells a story—about an individual and educator with *authority*.

Nancy, while a sophomore at Wellesley College and while I was in the Army in Germany, interviewed with the Roxbury Latin School on my behalf; I got the job. Two years later, while I was at a funeral, a chance comment to an Australian headmaster visiting Roxbury Latin that I was interested in teaching "abroad" led to that job offer. During our years in Cambridge, she started the raising of our four children, learned to read Chinese, received an M.A. in East Asian Studies at Harvard, co-edited a book on moral education with me, and taught part-time at what was then called the Cambridge High and Latin School.

When we moved to Andover, she joined the faculty at the newly coeducational Phillips Academy, serving as a history teacher, coach, academic adviser, dormitory supervisor, and carefully-in-the-shadows counselor to the headmaster, while knitting interwoven "A" size 2 sweaters for almost two dozen campus faculty babies and writing a secondary school textbook on Chinese history and a case book on moral decisions for high school students.

When we moved to Providence, I to teach at Brown, she joined the faculty at the Wheeler school as history instructor and department chair; she later also joined me in teaching a Brown course that "traveled" to schools in our region, we and the undergraduates shadowing high school students and writing portraits of revealing moments in those students' days.

In our recent years after her retirement from Wheeler and mine from Brown we have had the opportunity to work as one, as co-visitors to dozens of secondary schools (from which emerged her book on the high school senior year, *Crossing the Stage*) and then as Acting co-Principals of the Francis W. Parker Charter Essential School, of which we had been part of the group of founders. We co-authored *The Students Are Watching: Schools and the Moral Dilemma* and had the fun of enduring interviews together from the *NewsHour with Jim Lehrer* to the *Oliver North Show* and public conversations on that controversial topic.

Today we teach a course at Harvard together on secondary school design and at the New Teachers Collaborative, a school-based teacher education program based at the Parker Charter Essential School, and, in collaboration with Deborah Meier, we have prepared for Beacon Press a collection of "letters to parents" that Deborah at Mission Hill School in Boston and we while acting principals at Parker prepared weekly for our schools' families *(Keeping School: Letters to Families)*.

All this has been an extraordinary joy. That our four children, three children-in-law, and ten grandchildren have encouraged us in these unusual collaborations is a special blessing.

Three men in particular are owed special acknowledgment.

Two took substantial risks in offering me jobs. Sir Brian Hone, Headmaster of the Melbourne Church of England Grammar School in Australia, hired me in 1958 sight unseen (largely on the word of Nancy, whom he had briefly met). The year teaching in Victoria was an eye-opener, and the generosity of the Hones unbounded. Sir Brian assigned me "readings" from notables in British education and grilled me on them over meat pie lunches in his office.

Nathan Marsh Pusey, Harvard's President, asked me to be the Dean of the Graduate School of Education while I was at the tender age of thirty-one and only three years from the receipt of my Ph.D. He counseled and backed me during the tumultuous years of the 1960s, always ready with steady advice. A quiet, serious, wonderfully stubborn man, rarely the tactician but a brilliant strategist, he always took a long, principled, deeply humane view of the obligations of the scholarly community. He taught me much, about values and about courage.

Lawrence Cremin of Teachers College Columbia University was a mentor from the mid-1950s, encouraging my scholarship, setting me onto research of the nineteenth-century academy movement, counseling me in the special way that an outsider could during the years when I served as Dean and urging me at the end of the 1960s to apply for a Guggenheim Fellowship and to take my family overseas for a term.

One always must acknowledge luck. The sixth of six children, I was raised in a large and loving family. My military duties fell between two wars, I never faced hazards, and my superiors gave me opportunities beyond my rank. I became Dean at Harvard just as Federal aid to education started, making possible a range of high-risk initiatives impossible today. My hankering to get back to school work meshed with Phillips Academy's intention both to find a way to become a coeducational school and to sharpen the focus of its public mission, issues that I cared about. My early 1980s interest in high schools over-lapped with those of several key foundations, making it possible to mount a substantial research project. The need of Brown University for a senior appointment in Education and my search for both a job and a setting to launch what became the Coalition of Essential Schools came at once, and the willingness of President Howard Swearer and Professor Reginald Archambault to take me on was generous. My Brown colleagues and successive Presidents were stalwart in their support of what were then highly unusual arrangements for a small Education Department embedded in a liberal arts university.

Two school principals have profoundly influenced me over the past quarter century: Deborah Meier and Dennis Littky. They are progres-sives in the deepest sense and persons of enormous courage and per-sistence. No two practitioners have had and continue to have more influence over the way that truly concerned people think about school-ing and act upon that thought than have Deborah and Dennis. Further, they act: they *bear witness,* creating schools that have been and continue to be in the vanguard of secondary school reform.

At every post where I have worked I was blessed with strong col-leagues, numbering in the hundreds over fifty years. Some have had careers that happily intertwined with mine at several points along the way: Arthur and Barbara Powell, Edwin Campbell, Alixe Callen, Kathy Hardie, Rick Lear and Patricia Wasley, Robert McCarthy, Kath-leen Cushman, Paula and Rob Evans, Philip Zaeder and Sylvia Thayer, Jim Nehring, Larry Myatt, and Linda Nathan, Michael Shear and Laura Rogers especially among them.

Yale University Press published my first book, *Secondary Schools at the Turn of the Century,* in 1964. That the Press is publishing this book in 2004 is a special joy, and I am grateful to my friends there, to my editor Jonathan Brent, to my manuscript editor, Joyce Ippolito, and to my agent, Betsy Lerner, who as a Houghton Mifflin editor shepherded *Horace's School* to publication in 1992.

Notes

Preface: The Red Pencil

1. Nancy Sizer and I have recently written of a fourth "silence," one traditionally called "moral education" and perhaps better called "goodness" (or the lack
thereof) in schools: *The Students Are Watching: Schools and the Moral Contract*
(Boston: Beacon Press, 1999). The manner in which we adults visibly and au-
dibly interact with our students and the way that the school's organization
affects our and their lives is a powerful "curriculum," one about which school
authorities pay far too little attention.

2. David Tyack is responsible for the nice metaphor of *grammar* of schooling. A
recent use of it appears in his and Larry Cuban's *Tinkering Toward Utopia: A
Century of Public School Reform* (Cambridge: Harvard University Press, 1995),
chapter 4. *Regularities* is an equally useful word to describe schools' routines;
Seymour Sarason provided that expression in his *The Culture of the School and
the Problem of Change* (Boston: Allyn and Bacon, 1971), chapter 6. The word
system has variety of meanings in education, not all of them pejorative as I have
used it here. The world itself is a complex system, many parts dynamically
interconnecting, with enormous effect. Indeed, one does not understand our
world without recognizing and honoring this complexity of reciprocating connections; *systems thinking* must infuse the school's curriculum. See Peter Senge,
The Fifth Discipline, 3 volumes (New York: Doubleday, 1999/2000).

Chapter 1: Building

1. Bernard Bailyn, *Education in the Forming of American Society* (Chapel Hill: University of North Carolina Press, 1960), 9.
2. Ibid., 14.
3. James Q. Wilson (ed.), *The Metropolitan Enigma: Inquiries into the Nature and Dimensions of America's "Urban Crisis"* (Washington, D.C.: Chamber of Commerce of the United States, 1967).
4. Frederick Mosteller and Daniel P. Moynihan (eds.), *On Equality of Educational Opportunity* (New York: Random House, 1972), 5.
5. Ibid., 6.
6. Ibid., 7. Italics in the original.
7. Ibid., 20.
8. Ibid., 21.
9. Ibid., 22.
10. Edward C. Banfield, *The Unheavenly City: The Nature and the Future of Our Urban Crisis* (Boston: Little, Brown, 1968, 1970), 48ff.
11. Ibid., vii.
12. Theodore R. Sizer, *Horace's Compromise: The Dilemma of the American High School* (Boston: Houghton Mifflin, 1984), 143ff.
13. *Youth: Transition to Adulthood: Report of the Panel on Youth of the President's Science Advisory Committee,* James S. Coleman, chairman (Chicago: University of Chicago Press, 1974).
14. Milbrey McLaughlin, Merita A. Irby, and Juliet Langman, *Urban Sanctuaries: Neighborhood Organizations in the Lives and Futures of Inner-City Youth* (San Francisco: Jossey-Bass, 1994); Lisbeth B. Schorr, *Common Purpose: Strengthening Families and Neighborhoods to Rebuild America* (New York: Doubleday, 1997); Laurence Steinberg, *Beyond the Classroom: Why School Reform Has Failed and What Parents Need to Do* (New York: Simon and Schuster, 1996); Mihalyi Csikszentmihalyi and Barbara Schneider, *Becoming Adult: How Teenagers Prepare for the World of Work* (New York: Basic, 2000).
15. Steinberg, *Beyond the Classroom,* 184.
16. Robert D. Putnam, *Bowling Alone: The Collapse and Revival of American Community* (New York: Simon and Schuster, 2000), 296ff.
17. Lawrence A. Cremin, *Public Education* (New York: Basic Books, 1976), 3.
18. Ibid., 8.
19. Ibid., 30.
20. Ibid., 4. Italics in the original.
21. Todd Gitlin, *Media Unlimited: How the Torrent of Images and Sounds Overwhelms Our Lives* (New York: Metropolitan Books/Henry Holt, 2001), 16–17. Italics

in the original. The late Neil Postman of New York University was one of the first scholars to raise this issue in a series of books and articles published over the past three decades.

22. See Gene I. Maeroff, *A Classroom of One: How Online Learning Is Changing Our Schools and Colleges* (New York: Palgrave Macmillan, 2003).

23. Lawrence A. Cremin, *American Education: The Metropolitan Experience* (New York: Harper and Row, 1988), 361ff.

Chapter 2: Authority

1. The school was the Francis W. Parker Charter Essential School. See James Nehring, *Upstart Startup: Creating and Sustaining a Public Charter School* (New York: Teachers College Press, 2000).

2. The "treaties" metaphor is from Arthur G. Powell. See Arthur G. Powell, Eleanor Farrar, and David K. Cohen, *The Shopping Mall High School: Winners and Losers in the Educational Marketplace* (Boston: Houghton Mifflin, 1985), chapter 2.

3. Richard Sennett, *Authority* (New York: Knopf, 1980), 5.

4. Ibid., 179.

5. Theodore Sizer, *The Works of Colonel John Trumbull: Artist of the American Revolution*, revised edition (New Haven: Yale University Press, 1967).

6. Ibid., xii.

7. Ibid., 17.

8. Arthur G. Powell, *Lessons from Privilege: The American Prep School Tradition* (Cambridge: Harvard University Press, 1996).

9. Ibid., 245.

10. See Jacqueline Ancess, *Beating the Odds: High Schools as Communities of Commitment* (New York: Teachers College Press, 2003); and Thomas Toch, *High Schools On A Human Scale: How Small Schools Can Transform American Education* (Boston: Beacon Press, 2003).

Chapter 3: Order

1. David B. Tyack, *The One Best System: A History of American Urban Education* (Cambridge: Harvard University Press, 1974).

2. Horace Mann, *Twelfth Annual Report* to the Massachusetts State Board of Education (1848), as reprinted in Lawrence A. Cremin, *The Republic and the School: Horace Mann on the Education of Free Men* (New York: Teachers College Press, 1957), 87.

3. National Educational Association, *Report of the Committee of Ten on Secondary*

School Studies . . . (Washington, D.C.: Government Printing Office, 1893), reprinted as an appendix in Theodore R. Sizer, *Secondary Schools at the Turn of the Century* (New Haven: Yale University Press, 1964).

4. Ibid., 264ff.

5. Alfred North Whitehead, *The Aims of Education and Other Essays* (New York: Macmillan, 1929), 1.

6. Sizer, *Secondary Schools at the Turn of the Century,* 264–265.

7. *The Yale Report of 1828,* reprinted in Richard Hofstadter and Wilson Smith (eds.), *American Higher Education: A Documentary History* (Chicago: University of Chicago Press, 1961), 1:278; compare with the National Commission on Excellence in Education, *A Nation At Risk: The Imperatives for Educational Reform* (Washington, D.C.: Government Printing Office, 1983).

8. See Jerome Bruner, *The Process of Education* (Cambridge: Harvard University Press, 1960); Howard Gardner, *The Disciplined Mind: What All Students Should Understand* (New York: Simon and Schuster, 1999); David Perkins, *Smart Schools: From Training Memories to Educating Minds* (New York: Free Press, 1992); and Robert J. Sternberg, *Thinking Styles* (New York: Cambridge University Press, 1997).

9. See Diane Ravitch, *Left Back: A Century of Failed School Reforms* (New York: Simon and Schuster, 2000), chapter 9.

10. Mortimer J. Adler, *The Paideia Proposal: An Educational Manifesto* (New York: Macmillan, 1982), v.

11. Adler, *The Paideia Proposal,* 5–8.

12. *American Heritage Dictionary of the English Language,* 4th edition, s.v. "maieutic."

13. For example, the National Padeia Center at the University of North Carolina, Greensboro.

14. Adler, *Paideia Proposal,* back cover.

15. See Ravitch, *Left Back,* 47ff.

16. Peter L. Berger and Richard John Neuhaus, *To Empower People: The Role of Mediating Structures in Public Policy* (Washington, D.C.: American Enterprise Institute for Public Policy Research), 1. Italics in the original.

17. Ibid., 2. Italics in the original.

18. Ibid., 6.

19. Ibid., 21.

20. Ibid., 22. Italics in the original.

21. Deborah Meier, *In Schools We Trust: Creating Communities of Learning in an Era of Testing and Standardization* (Boston: Beacon Press, 2002).

22. Berger and Neuhaus, *To Empower People,* 41.

23. David S. Seeley, *Education through Partnership: Mediating Structures and Education* (Cambridge, Mass.: Ballinger/Harper and Row, 1981).

24. John E. Coons and Stephen D. Sugarman, *Education by Choice: The Case for Family Control* (Berkeley: University of California Press, 1978).

25. David Osborne and Ted Gaebler, *Reinventing Government: How the Entrepreneurial Spirit Is Transforming the Public Sector* (New York: Penguin, 1993).

26. White House Task Force on Cities, internal typescript, footnote 1.

27. Theodore R. Sizer and Phillip Whitten, "A Poor Children's Bill of Rights," *Psychology Today* (August 1968), 59, 63.

28. National Commission on Governing America's Schools, *Governing America's Schools: Changing the Rules* (Denver: Education Commission of the States, 1999).

29. Ibid., viii.

Chapter 4: Horace Compromised

1. The Study of High Schools was cosponsored by the National Association of Secondary School Principals and the National Association of Independent Schools. It was wholly funded by private foundations.

2. Arthur G. Powell, Eleanor Farrar, and David K. Cohen, *The Shopping Mall High School: Winners and Losers in the Educational Marketplace* (Boston: Houghton Mifflin, 1985).

3. Robert Hampel, *The Last Little Citadel: American High Schools since 1940* (Boston: Houghton Mifflin, 1986).

4. Ibid., ix.

5. Theodore R. Sizer, *Horace's Compromise: The Dilemma of the American High School* (Boston: Houghton Mifflin, 1984, 1985, 1992, 2004).

6. The Coalition of Essential Schools is now an independent, not-for-profit corporation headquartered in Oakland, California. Its work is largely decentralized to more than twenty regional centers.

7. Sizer, *Horace's Compromise*, 214ff. A tenth principle, on equity, was added in the 1990s.

8. Theodore R. Sizer, *Horace's School: Redesigning the American High School* (Boston: Houghton Mifflin, 1992).

9. Theodore R. Sizer, *Horace's Hope: What Works for the American High School* (Boston: Houghton Mifflin, 1996).

10. The list of critical, persuasive books is lengthy. Over the past four decades, for example, a comprehensive study was led by John Goodlad; his first major report appeared as *A Place Called School: Prospects for the Future* (New York: McGraw-Hill, 1984). A string of studies by Mihalyi Csikszentmihalyi and his colleagues, starting with *Being Adolescent: Conflict and Growth in the Teenaged Years* (New York: Basic, 1984) and most recently *Becoming Adult: How Teenagers Prepare for the World of Work* (New York: Perseus/Basic, 2000), has strengthened the

painful critique of the status quo. Most recently, Denise Clark Pope's *"Doing School": How We Are Creating a Generation of Stressed-Out, Materialistic, and Miseducated Students* (New Haven: Yale University Press, 2001) puts particular faces on students in a well-regarded but clearly dysfunctional public high school.

11. "Tinker" is not necessarily a perjorative, as David Tyack and Larry Cuban have argued from the vantage point of history. See Tyack and Cuban, *Tinkering toward Utopia: A Century of Public School Reform* (Cambridge: Harvard University Press, 1995).

12. Jim Cullen, *The American Dream: A Short History of an Idea That Shaped a Nation* (New York: Oxford University Press, 2002), 96. Punctuation in the original.

13. Harvard was one of the exceptions. It housed two major federally financed curriculum projects, Harvard Project Physics and Harvard Project Social Studies, and an ambitious, computer-based "information system for vocational decisions" for use by high and vocational schools. Faculty from the schools of Education, Arts and Sciences, Medicine, Public Health, and Divinity were deeply involved in the creation of and teaching at four new secondary schools—two within what is now called the Cambridge Rindge and Latin School (the Pilot and Cluster schools), one in Boston (the Robert W. White School) serving adolescents with special emotional needs, and one in Aiyetoro, Nigeria, in association with that nation's Western Region government. By the turn of the century, however, none of these schools survived, at least as originally designed. Project Physics, led by Gerald Holton, Professor emeritus of Physics, however, carries on independent of the university.

14. Bernard Bailyn, *Education in the Forming of American Society: Needs and Opportunities for Study* (Chapel Hill: University of North Carolina Press, 1960), 14.

Epilogue: Dodging Our Duty

1. There are dozens of books and studies about large-scale standardized testing. To my eye, the most succinct and, given the reputations of its authors, the most persuasive is the Congressionally mandated study by the National Research Council, *High Stakes: Testing for Tracking, Promotion, and Graduation* (Washington, D.C.: National Academy Press, 1999). A sophisticated recent study on testing in secondary schools is Martin Carnoy, Richard Elmore, and Leslie Siskin (eds.), *The New Accountability: High Schools and High Stakes Testing* (New York: Routledge, 2003).

2. See Thomas Toch, *High Schools on a Human Scale: How Small Schools Can Transform American Education* (Boston: Beacon Press, 2003), Jacqueline Ancess, *Beating the Odds: High Schools as Communities of Commitment* (New York: Teachers College Press, 2003), and Todd Oppenheimer, *The Flickering Mind:*

The False Promise of Technology in the Classroom and How Learning Can Be Saved (New York: Random House, 2003), chapter 11. There are articles and books on several experiments; on the Met Schools, for example, see Eliot Levine, *One Kid at a Time: Big Lessons from a Small School* (New York: Teachers College Press, 2002). Most of these schools are still in their infancy; only time will tell if they survive under the weight of tradition of what "high school is."

3. National Association of Secondary School Principals, Reston, Virginia, 1989 (Fourth printing of "Breaking Ranks"), 2003 ("Breaking Ranks II").